This book is a gift to those of us with d
friends who are Catholic. I do not knov
resource on Catholicism so careful to a
deeply committed to winning souls, nc
complexities. The issues are not simple. Chris Castaldo knows
firsthand the difficulties and possibilities, and he is a trustworthy
guide as we dream and pray and seek to speak with gentleness and
patience and clarity.

David Mathis, executive editor, desiringGod.org;
elder, Cities Church, Minneapolis

Talking with Catholics is vintage Castaldo – deeply pastoral,
generous to the other side, full of humor, and insightful about the
issues that really matter. The author finds the perfect balance of
truth and love. He doesn't misrepresent the Catholic Church, yet
he tests every claim by the Word of God. Castaldo has written a
book that anyone who loves a Roman Catholic friend or relative
should own. In a dialogue that is too often harsh and painful,
Talking with Catholics shows us how to be truly Christian.

Dr. Bryan Litfin, Professor of Theology,
Moody Bible Institute

This is an excellent guide for Evangelicals about how to relate to
Roman Catholics and share the gospel with them. Chris Castaldo
is well qualified for this task both by his own experience and
by his studies. He manages to convey the key points with great
clarity. Much to be recommended.

Tony Lane, Professor of Historical Theology,
London School of Theology

Chris Castaldo doesn't just write about the need for grace and
truth as we Protestants talk with Roman Catholics. I have seen
him model grace and truth in personal evangelism, discipleship,
and preaching. No matter what you know or don't know about
Catholicism, you can learn from his example and experience.

Collin Hansen, editorial director of The Gospel Coalition
and author of *Blind Spots: Becoming a Courageous,
Compassionate, and Commissioned Church*

Chris Castaldo's voice is a valuable one for evangelical Protestants. In this book he speaks as a man raised and nurtured in the Catholic Church, a careful student of ecclesial and theological history, and a Protestant pastor with a heart to shepherd people in the way of Christ and his Word. These various strands of his life coalesce here in a truly helpful "guide for Evangelicals" that points us toward more accurate understanding, more careful words, and more loving lives of witness among our Catholic friends and loved ones.

Kathleen Nielson, PhD, Director of Women's Initiatives,
The Gospel Coalition

In *Talking with Catholics about the Gospel*, Chris displays his keen understanding of church history and systematic theology, helping Evangelicals to understand and relate constructively to Catholics. This work is highly recommended.

Ralph E. MacKenzie, coauthor of *Roman Catholics and Evangelicals: Agreements and Differences*

What you hold in your hands is a rare gem of a book. The author, a former Catholic who is now an evangelical Protestant theologian, very humbly and faithfully addresses the central differences between Catholics and Evangelicals about grace and saving faith. Reading the first chapter alone will likely transform your own perspective if you will allow "grace and truth" to sink deeply into your heart! I wish every Evangelical former Catholic that I know would read this fair-minded book. I also hope my Catholic brothers and sisters will read this fine book and continue our important dialogue in good faith. Chris pulls no punches and writes with Christian love.

John H. Armstrong, President of ACT3
and author of *Your Church Is Too Small*

Writing with a clear mind and a warm heart, Chris Castaldo guides the reader through the complex and multifaceted world of Catholicism. If you have Catholic family or friends, are interested in sharing the gospel more effectively, or simply want to understand Catholicism better, you need this book.

Colin Smith, Senior Pastor, The Orchard

TALKING
WITH
CATHOLICS
ABOUT
THE GOSPEL

· A GUIDE FOR EVANGELICALS ·

Chris Castaldo

ZONDERVAN

Talking with Catholics about the Gospel
Copyright © 2015 by Christopher A. Castaldo

This title is also available as a Zondervan ebook. Visit www.zondervan.com/ebooks.

Requests for information should be addressed to:
Zondervan, 3900 Sparks Dr. SE, Grand Rapids, Michigan 49546

Library of Congress Cataloging-in-Publication Data

Castaldo, Chris, 1971-
    Talking with Catholics about the Gospel : a guide for evangelicals / Chris
Castaldo.
      pages cm
    Includes index.
    ISBN 978-0-310-51814-3 (softcover)
    1. Evangelicalism-Relations-Catholic Church. 2. Catholic Church-Relations-
Evangelicalism. 3. Catholic Church-Doctrines. I. Title.
BR1641.C37C36 2014
282-dc23   2014028736

Cover design: Michelle Lenger
Cover photography: Masterfile
Interior design: Matthew Van Zomeren

Printed in the United States of America

HB 11.30.2023

To Frank Iannone
1 Timothy 1:5

CONTENTS

CHAPTER SIX

ACKNOWLEDGMENTS

Without the support of family and friends this book would not have been written. First and foremost, I thank my wife, Angela, and our children, Luke, Philip, Simeon, Aliza, and David. Your sacrifice, patience, and unconditional love are treasured gifts.

Thanks to Mark Gilbert, Eduardo Echeverria, Matt Ferris, Timothy Larsen, Christine Litavsky, and Charles Raith for reading the manuscript and providing valuable advice.

Thanks to my friends Lon Allison, Mark Brucato, Leonardo De Chirico, Collin Hansen, Tony Lane, Ralph MacKenzie, Mike McDuffee, John Armstrong, and Peter Figliozzi for your encouragement and thoughtful interaction.

Thanks to my editors Madison Trammel, Ryan Pazdur, and Greg Clouse. It has been a pleasure to work together.

And most of all, thanks to the triune God — Father, Son, and Holy Spirit — for providing strength for today and bright hope for tomorrow. To you be the glory and honor forever.

INTRODUCTION

This book is about communicating the good news of Jesus Christ among Roman Catholic friends and loved ones. Saying this, however, raises the question of the purpose of such communication. Am I suggesting that we target Catholics for evangelism because they are categorically unsaved? Before I answer this question, let me say a few words about the perspective from which I am coming.

I write as an evangelical Protestant.[1] I am not among those who consider the Roman Catholic Church to be a cult. I regard it as a legitimate Christian tradition, unlike, for instance, the Jehovah's Witnesses and the Church of Latter-Day Saints (Mormons), because Catholicism subscribes to the Apostles' and Nicene Creeds. I also contend that there are valuable lessons that evangelical Protestants can learn from our Catholic friends. But with regard to the biblical gospel, I believe that the Catholic Church has complicated and confused the faith by which one believes in Christ and is saved.

I am commonly asked whether I believe Catholics "are going to heaven." I typically respond by saying that only God has infallible insight into the condition of someone's soul: "People look at the outward appearance, but the LORD looks at the heart" (1 Sam. 16:7). I then state that, in my estimation, there are a good number of Catholics who are genuinely born again, some of whom are my friends. On the other hand, many Catholics don't seem to know Christ (of course, this is also true of many Protestants). Such people may possess certain pieces of Christian tradition, but they have not personally appropriated the gospel — "that Christ died for our sins in accordance with the Scriptures, that he was buried, that he was raised on the third day" (1 Cor. 15:3–4). Among such people, we are compelled to share the good news.

There is another reason why we must articulate the good news among Catholics. It is the same purpose behind gospel communication in our Protestant churches each Sunday morning; or for that matter, it is the reason why I must preach to myself every day. Because the gospel is bigger than the moment of one's conversion, reaching forward to define and transform all of life, we must remind one another that Jesus Christ is Lord (2 Cor. 10:3–5; Col. 3:16). It is the enterprise of encouraging and exhorting ourselves to love Christ and hate sin, as it says in Hebrews 3:12–13: "See to it, brothers and sisters, that none of you has a sinful, unbelieving heart that turns away from the living God. But encourage one another daily, as long as it is called 'Today.'" Thus, sharing the gospel with Catholic friends or family does not presume to judge the authenticity of their faith. Rather, it highlights the vital importance of proclaiming salvation to the world as a matter of our evangelical identity.

But how do we do it? The following text of Scripture, in my humble opinion, should be at the forefront of our reflection: "And the Word became flesh and dwelt among us, and we have seen his glory, glory as of the only Son from the Father, full of *grace and truth*" (John 1:14 ESV, emphasis added). With a balance that can only be described as perfect, our Lord Jesus Christ embodied the virtues of grace and truth in full measure. In every conversation our Lord responded with the utmost charity and discernment, refusing to allow a humanly engineered wedge to separate these virtues. As men and women whose identities are founded in Jesus Christ, we now pursue this same balance as a central part of our calling.

It starts by recognizing that communicating redemptive truth is an activity of grace, because such truth liberates us from sin and death. When Paul the apostle stood in the midst of the Areopagus, for instance, he first "perceived" the Athenians' need for divine grace and then he spoke gospel truth (Acts 17:22).[2] It would have been ungracious for Paul to withhold the message of salvation among those who needed it. So it is for us.

Grace and truth should also mark the *manner* of our communication. How can we preach the message of grace in a graceless voice? Not only does such communication ring hollow, it becomes, according to the apostle, like "a noisy gong or a clanging symbol"[3]—dissonant, distracting, and irritating. Therefore, our approach to witness should reflect the sacrificial love of the gospel itself.

And we communicate truth *because of* grace and its surpassing beauty and worth. It's like walking from a dark cave into the bright sunshine of day. The contrast makes our eyes blink with amazement. So it is with conversion. After coming to Christ, we continue blinking, awestruck that we who were formerly lost are now light in the Lord. As years advance, our spiritual eyes begin to acclimate, but not fully. The same wonder of grace that we ourselves have received now motivates us to tell others.

Finally, concerning my particular treatment of this subject, I offer these few caveats. Because the sacraments are not at the leading edge of my theological vision, evangelical readers who are High-Church Anglican and Lutheran will occasionally have a different perspective from what I propose in these pages. It will also become obvious that I have been influenced by the Reformed tradition, particularly with respect to God's initiative in salvation. Finally, I write with full recognition that while evangelism among Catholic friends and loved ones is urgent, it can also be difficult, as our next chapter illustrates.

CHAPTER ONE

GRACE AND TRUTH

I t was a poor decision, probably the result of too much espresso. But then, I was in good company.

It all started at a Seattle's Best café in Chicago. In the warm glow of a fireplace, with the aroma of freshly ground beans wafting in the air, some college buddies and I were busy planning. The previous summer we had visited the Atlanta Olympics to perform street preaching at Centennial Park. Returning to our campus in the fall, we started "Student Outreach," an evangelism ministry to the pedestrians along and about Michigan Avenue, Chicago's busiest tourist thoroughfare.

The three of us sat there wondering, *Where can we find a captive audience?*

Out came the city map, followed by a long conversation about the relative merits of various locations. The subway was an obvious choice, if not for the screeching trains which always seemed to interrupt the conclusion of one's sermon. If only subway terminals didn't have trains.

After an hour of brainstorming, we had each exhausted the extent of our wisdom. Gathering our coats, we exited to the abnormally frigid November air. Immediately, we discovered a large crowd standing on the sidewalk, four or five people deep and stretching eastward toward Michigan Avenue. The sound of a thousand blended voices testified to its immensity. I turned to a woman with a scarf wrapped around her face and inquired, "Where's the party?"

"It's a funeral," she responded.

"For whom?"

Her look of incredulity said that I must be the most uninformed person in all of Chicago. Cardinal Joseph Bernardin, the city's archbishop, had died of cancer the previous Thursday. People the world over had come to whisper a final prayer and bid him farewell.

And indeed, it seemed as if the entire city of Chicago, Catholic and non-Catholic alike, was on the street that night. (Days later we'd learn that more than 100,000 visitors had come for the occasion.)

Astonishment gave way to a certain realization. I turned to my classmates. "What a large crowd."

"You might call them a captive audience," Jimmy responded.

Our eyes grew large with excitement. "You guys are nuts," said Steve. "Surely, you don't mean to preach outside the funeral."

"Steve, do you believe that God is all powerful?" Jimmy countered.

"Yes, but it's a funeral!"

16

No one spoke.

Low clouds from the west were bringing darkness early. I looked down at a dead leaf poking up through the snow; and then, with more drama than the moment required, I broke the silence. "People are headed toward eternal separation from God," I said, "and we have the message to save them. Shame on us if we don't preach the gospel."

GOING FORTH

The gauntlet was down. Hurrying back to campus for our gear, we dashed to our respective dorm rooms to grab paints, brushes, easel, paper, bungee cords, and a large stack of tracts.

"Are those all the tracts you're taking?" Jimmy asked. "You'd better grab another pile. We have the entire city waiting for us."

After stuffing everything into a couple of backpacks, we paused for a moment of prayer. Steve prayed, "Dear Lord, you say the harvest is plentiful and the laborers are few. We step forward this night as your servants, to proclaim your gospel. We wish to see your Spirit work through us to provide salvation to those who are lost. Would you do this? Amen."

In the growing winter darkness, we marched off to Holy Name Cathedral. I tried to imagine the various directions the evening could take. The optimist in me envisioned massive conversions; the realist in me, however, was fearful.

There was barely enough room for us on the sidewalk at our destination, which probably had something to do with our choice of location. The expectation of heaven or fear of hell couldn't adequately explain the audacity of our decision: the corner of State Street and Chicago Avenue was directly adjacent to the cathedral where Cardinal Bernardin's funeral was taking place. Literally a stone's throw from the church entrance, we were as close to the ceremony as was possible without getting arrested for disrupting the peace. There's a Yiddish word for such boldness: *chutzpah*.

While fastening the easel to a pole, the sound of cold engines idling on the street behind us filled my ears. The cars' exhaust was so thick you could taste it. This was a minor irritation, however, compared to the bone-cold chill in the air. Of course, this was Chicago. Citizens of northern Illinois have a winter code of conduct—you mustn't look cold, even if your toes feel as though they are detached from your feet. With this in mind, I turned to Jimmy:

"God created my Sicilian body for the Mediterranean. This is for the birds!"

"Yes, especially penguins," he responded.

People looked on curiously as we fastened the paint tray to the easel. The evening moon, pale through the clouds, hung above us as I stepped forward to preach the first sermon. Inspired by the nature of the occasion—a funeral—coupled with a class project I had recently completed on the topic of death in religious literature, I painted a crude picture of a tombstone, stepped beside the easel, and launched into my message:

Many people make it their policy to not talk about
death, even though it is certain to visit all of us. Our
lives move along a deathward trajectory that none of
us, even the most vigorous, can avoid. Not only do
thousands of people die each day, but death is the
horizon before which we rise from our pillows every
morning. The Italian playboy Casanova, for instance,
resented the thought of death because it threatened to
remove him from the stage of history before the end
of the show. Simone de Beauvoir suggested that death
instills anxiety precisely because it is "the inescapable
reversal of our projects."

Whatever the reason for one's aversion to death,
the fact remains that children continue to kneel beside
their beds and testify to its reality: "If I should die
before I wake, I pray thee, Lord, my soul to take."

My sermon continued, full of thinly veiled suggestions of how other Christian traditions were wrong. At
these points, I was speaking from resources acquired not
in the classroom or the library so much as from my own
experience as a disgruntled Catholic who had converted
to Evangelicalism. I never mentioned Catholicism explicitly, but it was quite obvious to what I was referring. The
amateur manner of these references was less than compelling, but it mattered not since the audience was captive: a
steady flow of humanity passed by me, one step at a time.
In the eyes of these Catholics, our homiletic display was
strange at best; but after listening for a bit, many became
incensed. A discernable tension hung in the air.

I concluded my message with a challenge:

Today's misery and helplessness is simply a foretaste of what awaits those who reject the Savior, Jesus Christ. He alone died and was raised from the grave, once and for all, our perfect sacrifice.

Everyone in the hearing of my voice, choose your epitaph this day. In what do you trust? Where will you find yourself after crossing the threshold of life into death? Turn to Jesus this evening and be saved!

A TOUGH CROWD

War is ugly, especially when you get in the trenches. On the field of battle, you look into people's eyes and see their intensity, their gnashing teeth, their angry hearts. The scenario before us was beginning to look like a war zone.

Farthest away, in the outer circle of the crowd, was a man with a large mustache and a leather jacket. "Go home, fanatic!" he yelled. Behind him was a cleric wearing an enamel lapel badge displaying a diocesan emblem. His mournful eyes — moist and sleepless — grabbed my attention. A woman wearing a large crucifix raised her hand and shouted, "May the Mother of God have pity on you!"

Closer to me, I spotted a nun wearing a traditional habit. When our eyes met, I could not easily dismiss the kindness in her face. I felt conflicted and puzzled over the strange mixture of responses.

A few other comments rang out, and then, for a moment, there was silence. It was as if we had all run out of breath or forgotten how to speak. I was aware that something needed to be said to defuse the situation, but I was at a loss for words. I still hadn't learned that there is a quality of communication that goes deeper than mere information — a way of speaking that conveys gentleness, even in the face of disagreement.

Frozen and disillusioned, I turned to Steve. "It's your turn." His face held an expression of dread as he swallowed hard and stepped forward. With the unpleasant fallout of my message in plain view, Steve decided to take a different approach. He replaced my tombstone art with a fresh piece of paper and proceeded to write two questions on it:

"How do you spell divine love?"
"What is the greatest gift?"

Wiser and more winsome than I, Steve sought to emphasize the gracious character of God. Pacing to and fro with his lanky arms extended, gesturing according to his characteristic rhythm, Steve punctuated each segment of his sermon with the same phrase, "What kind of love is this?" His raspy voice betrayed that he had a cold, which gave his words a forceful quality, like those of a radio broadcaster. I noticed that the crowd was listening with more ease and attentiveness than they had been previously. I wasn't sure where Steve's refrain would end, but it seemed to be working.

Midway through Steve's message, I stepped behind the crowd to see how our soap box appeared to onlookers. Did we seem earnest, vigorous, sincere, or just mad? Many would have probably labeled us as "fanatics," the sort of people who keep firearms beside their King James Bibles. Some walked by quickly, looking back with incredulity, whispering and pointing as they went.

As our skyscraper canyon funneled bitter gusts of wind from Lake Michigan, I tightened my coat and scarf. Each knifing draft made me resent Chicago more. Despite Gore-Tex gloves and insulated boots, my fingers and toes had become numb. In obedience to the instincts of my Italian body, I ambled over to a nearby White Hen Pantry to give my red cheeks and burning-cold hands a moment of reprieve.

I ordered three hot drinks and hoped that they would take a long time to make, and then I started to reflect more deeply on the responses to my sermon. With the friendly nun's face in my mind and Steve's refrain concerning love in my ears, I had a new thought: *How can we preach the realities of life and death with passion and urgency—and a life-giving spirit—and yet not sound irritating?*

Then another thought crossed my mind. It had been the subject of the previous Wednesday's biblical theology lecture—the concept that God *is* love. Professor Laansma had emphasized that *hesed*, the Hebrew word used most frequently in the Old Testament to describe God's love, often translated as "loving-kindness" or "steadfast love," is a selfless love, one that looks out for others regardless of the circumstances. It then dawned on me—the realization that my preaching had expressed grace in a graceless voice, a message of divine love conspicuously devoid of affection.

Just as my slow-running blood was starting to flow normally again, the guy behind the counter returned with our three coffees and, after loading them into a carry tray, I returned to the frosty tundra outside.

SHARING GRACE *AND* TRUTH

I found that Steve had completed his message and Jimmy was now beginning. A nervous sensation ran through my body. Jimmy, who had been a linebacker in high school, tended to approach street preaching like he did football: straightforward, taking no prisoners. Under the dictionary definition of "confrontational evangelism" was surely a picture of Jimmy holding a paint brush.

As Jimmy started to make distinctions between "true and false faith," I cringed. In front of him were some particularly large men; the Four Horsemen of the Apocalypse had nothing on these guys. One of them stared at Jimmy, looking perplexed, as if he were unsure of whether he wanted to throw a punch or pray. In the meantime, Jimmy continued speaking, apparently oblivious to the situation.

Fortunately, the Four Horsemen kept walking. The real challenge came behind them: a priest with fire in his eyes was obviously outraged by the whole ordeal. In response to Jimmy's sermon, he turned to the people surrounding him and proceeded to recite the Hail Mary. "Recite" isn't the right word. It was more like shouting. Jimmy, the consummate testosterone-filled alpha male, couldn't possibly surrender, so he raised his voice. The result was a shouting match between the rosary-wielding priest and the paintbrush-waving Bible student. Steve, always the peacemaker, looked horrified.

Thankfully, the antiphonal shouting didn't last long. The line, which was now moving faster, ushered the priest and his parishioners beyond us. Deep down in the pit of my stomach I regretted what had transpired and decided that it was time to call it a night. I looked into the faces of Steve and Jimmy, who read my mind and responded, "Yeah, I think it's time to go."

As I was packing up the easel, a man wearing a fedora and black scarf, whose wrinkled face revealed his age, approached me with outstretched hand and introduced himself as Monsignor Morris.

"Please understand," he said, "the suggestion that we Catholics are outside of Christ and that your particular denomination has the corner on truth is difficult to swallow. Let me encourage you to remain excited for Jesus, and, at the same time, equally committed to loving people, for these are the two great commandments—to love God and love your neighbor."

With that, the monsignor smiled and walked off.

Upon returning to campus, Jimmy, Steve, and I parted company, left alone with heads full of memories of the previous hours. "Conflicted" is the best word to describe how I felt—happy to have stepped out in faith, but dissatisfied with the outcome. I slept very little that night. More than anything, my thoughts shifted between Steve's sermon, the nun, and the parting thought of Monsignor Morris.

A wider and deeper scrutiny is necessary to understand all that happened that day outside Holy Name Cathedral. On one level, it was simply a few college sophomores doing street preaching; but it was more than that. It was also a clash of two worlds: Catholic and Protestant, each with its own theology, worldview, and culture. Insight into these differences, guided by Scripture, is essential if we are to successfully proclaim Christ and avoid unnecessary strife. The following chapters seek to navigate the complexities of this challenge.

CHAPTER TWO

UNDERSTANDING CATHOLICS

Perspective is never shaped in a vacuum. We all live in some context where uninvited forces impose themselves, leading us to raise particular sets of questions, to embrace certain assumptions, and to recognize value in some ideas and not others. To travel the path of religious discussion without occasionally stepping back to evaluate how forces such as education, culture, ethnicity, and experience influence one's views (especially our own views) is tantamount to watching a puppet show without recognizing that there is a puppeteer in the background.

The purpose of this chapter is to peel back the curtain of underlying values that guide Catholic belief and practice. We begin by looking at the term "evangelical" to get a sense of our own religious identity and priorities. We then consider the three main types of Catholics in America — traditional, evangelical, and cultural — with reference to the forms of authority on which each belief system is built. Once the salient features of these Catholic profiles are identified, we will then explore strategies for approaching people in each category in conversation about the gospel. Finally, we will conclude with an exercise for evaluating our assumptions.

Given the frequency with which we use the term "evangelical," it is important to explain what this author has in mind by it. British scholar David Bebbington has famously proposed that "evangelicalism" is a spiritual movement of the Protestant tradition which originated in mid-eighteenth century Britain around four emphases: conversion, activism, the Bible, and the cross.[1] While lively debate surrounds how much this time period is in continuity with preceding centuries of evangelical renewal, there appears to be a general acceptance of Bebbington's portrait.[2]

Historian Elisabeth Jay explains why it is difficult to define the term "evangelical," suggesting it is largely due to the revivalist origins of the movement in which elements of doctrine, piety, and organization were shaped by a wide array of leading personalities.[3] Jay writes, "The nickname 'Evangelical' was acquired by these men because of the zeal they showed in spreading the Evangel or Gospel."[4] Similarly, as Bebbington,[5] David Newsome,[6] and Sheridan Gilley[7] have argued, each particular leader and his or her surrounding circumstances effectively broadened the meaning of the term.[8] The following sampling of individuals and their contributions is simply intended to offer a sense of the movement's general complexion and to portray the contours of the tradition.

The revivals of John Wesley and George Whitefield in the middle of the eighteenth century brought
an increased emphasis on personal faith to the working
class of Britain. It was decades later when the upper class
and segments of the established church were also affected
by such renewal. This was especially so between the
years 1790–1830 when a "Calvinistic" brand of Evangelicalism acquired a significant following (often linked
to Whitefield). These early Evangelicals distinguished
themselves with amazing stories of conversion. One such
example is John Newton (1725–1807), the slave trader
turned minister and hymn writer who penned "Amazing
Grace" and "How Sweet the Name of Jesus Sounds."[9]
Wherever the movement existed, a concern to embody
and proclaim the gospel message, with a view to conversion, was central.

Space will not permit listing all of the individuals
who contributed to early Evangelicalism's impact, but I
will highlight several. Some were scholarly, such as Isaac
Milner (1750–1820) and Charles Simeon (1759–1836),
whose work infused Cambridge University with an
evangelical awareness. The so-called Clapham Sect,
consisting of wealthy individuals including John Venn
(1759–1833), Henry Thornton (1760–1815), and William Wilberforce (1759–1833), engaged the enterprise
of social reform, eventually effecting the abolition of
slavery in the British Empire. In a similar vein was the
prison reformer, John H. Howard (1726–1790), and
the Seventh Earl of Shaftesbury, Anthony Ashley Coo-
per (1801–1885), who tirelessly served the poor and

oppressed. Evangelicals created their own publications such as the *Christian Observer, The Christian Guardian*, and the *Record*.[10] They also spawned a host of missionary societies, starting most notably with the Baptists in 1792.[11] The famous Sunday school movement, initiated by Hannah More (1745–1833) and popularized by Robert Raikes (1735–1811), is also part of the evangelical legacy. The list of such contributions is long.[12] Despite its varied and complex shape, Evangelicals shared a common identity, amorphous as it might be.

According to the evangelical Bishop of Liverpool, J. C. Ryle, it was "no written creed, no formal declaration of principles" that defined "Evangelical Religion."[13] With reference to evangelical leaders who preceded him, particularly to those of the late eighteenth century,[14] Ryle enumerates five values that properly identified the movement:[15]

1. Absolute supremacy of Holy Scripture
2. Appreciating the depth and prominence of human sinfulness
3. Paramount importance assigned to the work and office of the Lord Jesus Christ
4. The inward work of God's Spirit in the heart of man
5. Outward and visible work of the Holy Ghost

The English biographer, memoirist, and liberal politician, George W. E. Russell, offers a similar portrait. While he was a High Churchman, Russell recollected his childhood experience of Evangelicalism, noting in particular how the religion of his youth generally divided humanity into two categories: the "converted" ones, who had "closed with the offer" (and were thus assured of their salvation), and those of "an unconverted character."[16] The distinguishing characteristic of the first category, the "real" Christian, according to evangelical parlance, was one's heartfelt response to the gospel message. In Russell's words, "[I]f only we would accept the offer of salvation so made, we were forgiven, reconciled, and safe. The acceptance was 'Conversion.'"[17]

While numerous differences exist between eighteenth-century Britain and twenty-first century America, the commonalities between Evangelicalism then and now are noteworthy.[18] At the core is a shared commitment to defining oneself by the proclamation of the gospel message. Yet there are evangelical Anglicans who cherish formal liturgy and evangelical Baptists who don't. There are evangelical Calvinists who maintain eternal security and evangelical Wesleyans who believe that salvation can be lost. There are even some today who identify themselves as "evangelical Catholics."[19] What shall we say; have these different applications of the term depleted its meaning? Not necessarily.

With the above portrait in mind, we can at least have a sense of the central priorities of Evangelicalism. And I think we can do better than that. Doctrinal statements such as the Lausanne Covenant drafted in 1974 offer basic doctrinal underpinnings. Because Lausanne drew Christian leaders to Switzerland from around the world, it also has the advantage of representing an international range of thought. The combined input from non-Western scholars and practitioners makes it well-rounded, substantive, and readable. You may access the document in appendix 3.

Having some understanding of the term "evangelical," we now turn our attention to the different types of Catholics in the United States of America today: traditional, evangelical, and cultural. Before doing so, however, we must realize that these are general designations. The actual shape of Catholicism is varied and complex, as Catholic author, Peter Feuerherd, explains in his book *Holyland USA*:

> In reality, Catholicism includes those with disparate authority and opinions about almost everything under the sun. There are liberal bishops and conservative bishops. The pope sometimes differs with his own Curia. American Catholic voters are regularly viewed by experts as a crucial swing group in every national election, too diffuse to truly categorize. In fact, some scholars of religion refer to Catholicism as the Hinduism of Christianity, because it is infused with so many different schools of prayer, ritual, and perspective, much like the native and diverse religions of India now referred to under the single rubric of Hinduism.[20]

We can easily focus on the clerical attire of priests, common liturgical forms, and the ecclesial symbols that comprise parish life and reach the conclusion that the Catholic Church is perfectly unified. This, however, would be a superficial observation. When one looks below the surface, whether at particular religious orders or at the difference between liberal and conservative priests, one finds a great deal of variety.

TRADITIONAL CATHOLICS

"Traditional" Catholics (sometimes called "tradition-alists" or "ultra-traditional") base their faith chiefly on teachings and attitudes of the Church that predate Vatican II (1962–1965). You'll recall that Vatican II was the ecumenical council of the previous century in which the Church "opened the windows," as Pope John XXIII described it, to allow the fresh air of modern thought to stimulate renewal and to update a variety of traditional practices. For example, the Latin Mass would now be celebrated in the vernacular; priestly formation, religious freedom, ecumenism, and the calling of the laity were promoted; Bible study was encouraged, as was a more personal approach to faith. The "traditional Catholic," however, has a religious understanding and practice that stands in contrast to much of this.

George Weigel, in his book, *Evangelical Catholicism: Deep Reform in the 21st-Century Church*, describes the traditional Catholic as "Counter-Reformation Catholicism." He writes:

> Through a process of historical and theological evolution, the Catholicism of the Counter-Reformation came to understand the Church, and relationships within the Church, by analogy to a pyramid. The pope reigned at the apex of the structure; bishops,

priests, and vowed religious occupied the pyramid's middle tiers; the lay faithful manned the bottom. Authority flowed down the pyramid—and so, most of the time, did discussion. Thus Counter-Reformation Catholicism came to conceive the Bishops of Rome as the chief executive of a global enterprise whose local leaders (the bishops) were, in effect, papal delegates (or branch managers) for their respective areas; this, it was thought, was the appropriate embodiment of Catholic unity and apostolicity for the early modern age.[21]

Weigel goes on to explain how this conception of the Church tended to "crowd out the rich array of images that earlier embodiments of the Church had drawn from the Bible." Holiness of the Church institution, eucharistic adoration, and devotional practices focused on Mary and the Saints became central features of religious life. Unfortunately, discipleship through a regular encounter with the Bible was pushed to the periphery, if not absent altogether. If we were to portray this kind of Catholic, he or she would have the following tendencies:

- Discomfort with the personal dimensions of faith
- Exaltation of the Church institution
- Superstition and syncretism (customs such as regularly praying to dead relatives)
- Antipathy toward Protestantism
- An aversion to personal Bible study

Effective communication with traditional Catholics requires an understanding of the above values. In view of them, here are a few suggestions for engaging such a person in discussion about your faith:

- Abstain from unnecessary criticism of Catholic clergy. (This is always a good policy.)
- Slow and steady wins the race. Yes, the world needs prophets who are forthright. But when we engage traditional Catholics in the spirit of John the Baptist yelling "Repent!" we will repel them. Yes, we ought to speak with urgency, but such communication must be measured.
- Scripture is the appointed means by which God extends redemption to the world (Rom. 10:17). But there are ways of applying Scripture that impart life; or, if spoken carelessly (such as when we seek to win the argument without concern for a person's soul) can do harm. We must promote the former and avoid the latter.
- Because some traditional Catholics regard Protestants as being "off their nut," it is helpful to approach these loved ones with an emphasis on establishing credibility and rapport. Such a relational foundation goes a long way toward enriching conversations.
- Find areas of common ground. A prime example is the celebration of holidays. During Christmas we remember Jesus' incarnation and on Easter we celebrate the resurrection. On these occasions, common to our traditions, we can ask Catholic friends to educate us about their customs and

traditions. Such genuine interest will serve your understanding of your friend's Catholic faith, and, as conversation develops, it may also open the door for you to explain the gospel.

THE EVANGELICAL CATHOLIC

Many historians look to Pope Paul VI (pontificate 1963–1978) as the figure most responsible for shaping the evangelical Catholic identity, particularly in his exhortation titled *Evangelii nuntiandi*. The pontiff's statement emphasizes the lay-empowered impulse of Vatican II in terms of the role of every Catholic (not simply ordained priests) in spreading the message of Christian faith. In his exhortation, the pope begins by discussing the role of Jesus Christ as the great Evangelizer, the One who proclaimed the coming of the kingdom of God and testified to its reality. Those who embrace Jesus enter the family of faith, a community dedicated to embodying and proclaiming the Christian message. This, according to the pope, is the essential mission of the Church. In his words, "Evangelizing is in fact the grace and vocation proper to the Church, her deepest identity."[22] In this way, the entire Church is called to practice evangelism.

The pontiff's statement reflects the heartbeat of the evangelical Catholic. If we were to enumerate this category's distinctive traits, it would consist of the following:

- An appreciation for the personal dimensions of faith

- A view of Jesus that is just as personal as it is sacramental
- A vibrant and "charismatic" experience of faith
- A willingness to relate to Protestants as brothers and sisters in Christ
- A routine of personal Bible study

In view of these qualities, here are some suggestions to keep in mind when relating to evangelical Catholics:

- Unlike the "traditional," the evangelical Catholic is outspoken about his or her faith. Therefore, it is entirely possible that this individual will seek to convert you to Catholicism. Rejoice! You are dealing with a friend who believes that doctrinal truth is important. Thus, the stage is set for a fruitful conversation in which both parties pursue a deeper encounter with Christ. Encourage such friends when you hear them speak truth, and when something sounds amiss, respond as instructed in 1 Peter 3, with "gentleness and respect."
- Because the Bible is a common commitment, there is good reason to consider conducting an investigative Bible study with your evangelical Catholic friend. Gatherings of this nature are a regular part of organizations such as Bible Study Fellowship and Neighborhood Bible Studies (now called "Q Place"). You might invite your friend to visit a nearby coffee shop on a weekly basis to look at the gospel of Mark or Paul's letter to the Romans.

- The word "charismatic" in Catholic circles is closer to the adjective "evangelical" in Protestantism. It underscores the Bible-centered, personal nature of faith more than the exercise of particular spiritual gifts. Still, the charismatic gifts are sometimes part of the life of a Catholic parish. If you happen to be a charismatic Protestant, you will find a great deal of common ground here.
- I belong to a men's group called New Canaan Society. Every week about fifty guys gather for coffee, prayer, and a testimony from a Christian brother. Some of these men are Catholic. What binds us together? It is regard for God's Word, prayer, and the belief in supernatural conversion — that God steps into human lives to bring about his new creation. This common bond illustrates the nature of evangelical Catholicism.

THE CULTURAL CATHOLIC

When I think of a cultural Catholic, I picture someone such as Ted Kennedy. After reading the late senator's autobiography, *True Compass: A Memoir*, I was struck by how ardent one can be in one's Catholic identity while having so little theological substance. For instance, Kennedy mentions his Catholicism hundreds of times, but he seems to have in mind its cultural heritage rather than its doctrinal beliefs and practices. Nevertheless, he insists that his faith was responsible for giving shape and direction to his political life. Here is how he describes it:

> My own center of belief, as I matured and grew curious about these things, moved toward the great Gospel of Matthew, chapter 25 especially, in which he calls us to care for the least of these among us, and feed the hungry, clothe the naked, give drink to the thirsty, welcome the stranger, visit the imprisoned. It's enormously significant to me that the only description in the Bible about salvation is tied to one's willingness to act on behalf of one's fellow human beings.[23]

It is incredible to see a Catholic of so many years, who would have heard the Scriptures read at countless Masses, claiming that the Bible contains only *one* passage which addresses the subject of salvation. But the above quotation indicates something more profound of the author's detachment from his faith. When he says that "he calls us to care for the least of these among us," Kennedy never identifies the subject of the pronoun "he." It turns out that the name of Jesus is entirely absent from the memoir.

In light of the above, here is a list of how cultural Catholics, such as Kennedy, compare to the other Catholic profiles:

- Faith is a private matter
- "Truth" lacks objective character and is relative to one's personal preferences
- Catholic "faith" may be a product of one's ethnic or familial background

- Personal beliefs trump biblical or magisterial authority
- Evangelicals are generally considered to be hopelessly narrow and divisive

Taking into account these religious commitments, here are some suggestions to guide your conversations with cultural Catholics:

- Because cultural Catholics tend to view faith as private and theology as largely irrelevant, attempts to explain doctrine to a cultural Catholic may make you feel like you are feeding steak to a duck. For example, a recent survey by sociologists at Catholic University, led by William D'Antonio, reported that a whopping 88 percent of Catholics in America believe that "how a person lives is more important than whether he or she is Catholic."[24] This is the cultural Catholic impulse. Because these individuals consider personal beliefs to be more significant than Church teaching, religious authority is largely disregarded. Therefore, when talking with a cultural Catholic, instead of presenting what sounds to you like scintillating doctrinal reflection (and to your cultural Catholic friend like a pedantic lecture), it is valuable to think in terms of personal testimonies. By embedding doctrinal truth in your experiences of Christ (e.g., how the Lord answered prayer or provided peace in a time of need) you are helping your cultural Catholic friend to develop mental categories for understanding the significance of historic Christian thought.

- Ted Kennedy is a good example of how Catholicism can be a function of one's ethnic or familial heritage. Keep in mind, however, that pointing to the shallowness of a cultural Catholic's faith — regardless of how conspicuous — may be interpreted not only as a personal critique but as an insult to one's familial background. A positive approach that concentrates on the redemptive love of Jesus is preferable.

- There is a good chance that our cultural Catholic friend, from his limited understanding of Christian faith, will assert that truth is socially constructed and relative. When this is the case, it is difficult to have discussions about doctrine. Therefore, we might give the relationship time to develop and allow life's circumstances to take their natural course. Hopefully, when your friend encounters a crisis (which eventually happens to us all) or religious questions arise in his mind, he will give you the privilege of serving him with the gospel. In such moments there tends to be greater receptivity to God's love.

EVALUATING YOUR POSTURE

It is not enough to simply understand what Catholics are like. We must also pause to consider the attitude and posture with which we relate to them. In other words, how do I trace the lines of commonality and difference among Catholics and Protestants, and how does this outlook inform my approach to conversation?

Missiologist Jim Hatcher has served in the heavily Catholic country of Austria for many years. Out of that experience, he has been able to recognize and articulate the nuanced positions that Evangelicals adopt toward Catholicism, creating a helpful rubric for categorizing those perspectives. As you look at the seven categories he has defined in the extract that follows, think about which best describes your own approach to your Catholic friends and loved ones.

EVANGELICALS AND CATHOLICS: A TAXONOMY OF PROTESTANT APPROACHES[25]

1. ACTIVELY ANTI-RC

Evangelicals with an actively "anti-RC approach" emphasize the teaching and practices of the Roman Catholic Church that they feel are contrary to biblical teaching. The errors of these teachings and practices are felt to be so substantial and fundamental that most Evangelicals with this approach feel it is virtually impossible to be both a born-again Christian and a practicing member of the RC Church. Churches and individuals with this approach feel that it is important to regularly and decisively explain these differences. Contact with Roman Catholics is generally limited to evangelizing and public polemic, in which the perceived errors of RC teaching and practice are exposed.

2. PASSIVELY ANTI-RC

Evangelicals with a "passively anti-RC" approach share the convictions of those above concerning the teachings and practices of the RC Church. They generally do not, however, use the public square to critique those teachings and practices. While there tends to be a strong desire to clarify distinctives among themselves, contact with Roman Catholic institutions is avoided and contact with RC members is generally limited to evangelism.

3. CO-EXISTENT

Those Evangelicals with a "co-existent" approach are concerned not to antagonize Roman Catholics by openly criticizing the RC Church, its teachings, or its practices. Many Evangelicals with this approach rarely concern themselves with doctrinal issues of any sort, including those that relate to Catholics. When differences are evident, they are seldom addressed. These Evangelicals' posture is best described by the word "ambivalence."

4. POSITIVE IDENTITY

Evangelicals with a "positive identity" approach to Roman Catholics are relatively open about their theological distinctives, while avoiding unnecessary criticism of the RC Church. Common ground is sought, as is positive contact with Roman Catholics and RC institutions. While cautious, these Evangelicals are open to cooperating with RCs in isolated social projects such as "pro-life" efforts and disaster relief. They would hesitate, however, to cooperate evangelistically since they reject both the institution and authority of the RC Church as well as certain central doctrines. Less central differences, as perceived by these Evangelicals, tend to be minimized.

5. SYMBIOTIC

Evangelicals with a "symbiotic" approach, while maintaining core distinctives, welcome and may even seek cooperation with Roman Catholics on multiple fronts. As with the "co-existent" approach, differences are seldom the subject of internal teaching or public debate. By contrast, however, resources and energy are expended to actively pursue positive points of contact, publicly underscoring common beliefs and practices and supporting common causes, including cooperation with "believing" Catholics in evangelistic efforts. Evangelicals with this approach do not want to be perceived as "competing" with RC institutions.

6. ECUMENICAL

Evangelicals with an "ecumenical" approach actively seek to build bridges with Roman Catholics in pursuit of unity. Evangelism among active RCs is discouraged, and common ground is the subject of both public proclamation and in-house teaching. Differences are generally perceived to be a matter of preference, historical and cultural, rather than theological and fundamental.

7. INTERNAL RENEWAL

Evangelicals with an "internal renewal" approach toward Roman Catholics seek to work within the RC Church and its institutions. Their desire is to encourage renewal with the goal of restoring "prodigal" RCs both to personal faith and to the RC Church. Their focus is often evangelism and personal discipleship through Bible study under the authority of, or at least in cooperation with, the local RC priest and parish. Divisive distinctions in teaching or practice are avoided or minimized.

Sometimes when I am teaching, I like to present these categories and then ask folks to raise their hands to indicate the viewpoint to which they belong. The response is extraordinary. Congregants who have known one another for years, even decades, and who are intimately familiar with the details of one another's lives, will look across the room in utter incredulity at their different perspectives on Catholicism: "You believe that?" I have seen elders actually get into an argument over the question. Here is the point: Evangelicals who otherwise agree on issues of doctrine are often at great variance over the question of how to view the Catholic Church.

A GOD-FOCUSED VISION

This side of glory, evangelical Protestants will often differ in their perspectives on Catholicism. However, there is something on which we can all agree, namely, the need to emulate God. "Be imitators of God," writes Paul in Ephesians 5. Because God is tri-personal—Father, Son, and Holy Spirit—he is the consummate model of relational life and peace. To be sure, divine persons who exist from eternity must relate in ways that fallen creatures can't imagine. Nevertheless, because we are made in God's image, to say nothing of the divine love that has been poured into our hearts (Rom. 5:5), we may confidently assert that loving others is central to our identity and calling. Indeed, this is why Jesus replied to the question about the greatest commandment by saying, "Love the Lord your God with all your heart and with all your soul and with all your mind" (Matt. 22:37). Then he added, "And the second is like it: 'Love your neighbor as yourself' " (Matt. 22:39). It is also why Jesus said, "By this all people will know that you are my disciples, if you have love for another" (John 13:35 ESV). Indeed, Jesus went so far as to say, "Love your enemies and pray for those who persecute you" (Matt. 5:44).

Why is this so important to remember? I am afraid that our posture toward Catholicism sometimes overlooks the imperative to love. Over and against this error, the great American theologian Jonathan Edwards (1703–1758) argued in his book, *The Nature of True Virtue*, that Christians must assign the appropriate measure of value to people and relationships.[26] Because men and women are made in God's image, they possess supreme dignity, value, and worth. When we fail to honor this worth, even in the midst of sharp disagreement, we dishonor the God in whose image all people are made.

Augustine (354–430) takes the idea further. His famous treatment of the Trinity develops the theme of love with reference to Godhead. Accordingly, Augustine asserted that genuine love always involves three elements: a lover, the one who is loved, and the love itself. God the Father is the lover, God the Son is the beloved, and God the Holy Spirit is the love that binds them together.[27] From this pattern, Augustine explains a practical implication of the fact that "God is love" (1 John 4:8): such love not only leads us heavenward in worship; it simultaneously inspires commitment to serving other people, even those with whom we disagree. Anything less is sub-Christian.

In our next chapter we look more closely at the beliefs and priorities of Catholic thought by tracing Roman Catholicism's story from the sixteenth-century Reformation to the present. Without being overly detailed, I hope to portray its broad contours in the interest of understanding reasons for the Catholic Church's contemporary form and mode of operation. Such insight will help us to avoid the tendency toward misguided caricatures and will fortify discussions of faith with a greater measure of credibility.

CHAPTER THREE

CATHOLIC HISTORY SINCE THE SIXTEENTH CENTURY

When we think of the Reformation of the sixteenth century, it is important to remember that it began as a Catholic movement of internal renewal.[1] We often look to 1517, the year when Luther nailed his Ninty-Five Theses to the church door at Wittenberg, as the Protestant Reformation's starting point.[2] We must bear in mind, however, that Luther was not intending to leave the Catholic Church in 1517. A cursory reading of the Theses reveals Luther's deference to the pope. Evidently, Luther believed that if the pontiff were only aware of the abuses occurring in Germany, he would have surely brought reform. He wrote in thesis 50, for instance: "If a pope knew how much people were being charged for an indulgence — he would prefer to demolish St. Peter's." It wasn't until 1521, the year Luther was excommunicated, that division was made explicit.

Spiritual reform was on the rise at this time in the Church. In the opening address at the Fifth Lateran Council (1512–1517), the Augustinian Cardinal, Giles of Viterbo (1469–1532), declared: "Men must be changed by religion, not religion by men."[3] Such "religious uneasiness," common to the whole of Europe at the start of the sixteenth century, sent thoughtful Christians to reexamine the roots of their faith.[4] This examination produced a wide range of proposals aimed at stimulating renewal, the form of which differed depending on region and time period.

The impulse toward Catholic reform was due to several factors. These included:

- an abysmal standard of morality by Pope Alexander VI and his Borgia family on whom he had lavished abundant privilege and wealth;[5]
- the Medici papacies which had made the city of Rome into a veritable haven of humanism;
- ongoing conflict between the Catholic Emperor, Charles V, and his popes;
- the popularizing of democratic ideals by public intellectuals such as Erasmus;
- dissemination of such ideals by the recently invented printing press;
- and, eventually, the distribution of Protestant tracts that questioned the accuracy of Catholic Church doctrine.

In the pages that follow, I will trace the broad outline of this narrative from the sixteenth century to the
present in the hope of understanding why contemporary
Catholics and Protestants are so different.

GETTING THE HOUSE IN ORDER

The Catholic Church of the early sixteenth century had
noteworthy features. With its accumulation of wealth it
wielded a great deal of secular power, particularly in its
governance of the Papal States. Clergy and laity lived
vastly different lives. For instance, they operated under
a different legal system (canon versus secular law), language (in the context of worship priests spoke Latin),
and numerous superficial differences, such as one's
haircut (clergy usually had a tonsure). Most laypersons
rarely received communion (typically one to three times
a year), and only under the "species" of bread, that is,
by receiving the consecrated wafer. Clergy on the other
hand, enjoyed partaking of the bread *and* the wine, often
doing so daily. The practice of pastoral care had not yet
come of age; therefore, one would rarely see his priest
outside of formal religious services. Because a significant
amount of the clergy was illiterate, especially outside
of urban centers, preaching and teaching tended to be
sub-biblical. And where the teaching ascended to greater
heights, the use of Latin made such teaching inaccessible
to most of the faithful.

In view of these problems, it was on the grassroots
level that many Catholics sought to reform the Church.

This happened in groups such as "The Oratory of Divine Love" (also called the "Theatines"), an informal society of devout Catholics who were dedicated to improving moral life in Rome and beyond.[6] There were also the "Barnabites," or "Clerks Regular of St. Paul," whose members preached, heard confessions, and visited hospitals.[7] The Capuchins, which started as an attempt to renew the Franciscan Order, also arose during this period.[8] In the upper echelons of Church authority was the *Spirituali*, which included prelates, intellectuals, and noblewomen.[9] So influential was this group that none other than Michelangelo is said to have experienced an evangelical form of renewal by their ministry.[10] Out of this soil a range of reformation efforts were born, some of which resulted in people disassociating themselves from the Roman Church (as in Protestantism) while others chose to remain under its authority.

In response to the building chorus of dissent, the Roman Church eventually called a council which met (mostly) in the northern Italian city of Trent on and off over the course of eighteen years (1545–1563). In addition to numerous initiatives for internal reform, such as elevating the level of education for priests and curbing clerical abuses, two major issues raised by Protestants were addressed by the Council Fathers: the nature of Christian authority and the doctrine of justification (that is, the way in which sinful humanity is accepted by God). With regard to the former, the Council of Trent concluded that Scripture and tradition both constitute God's word.[11] Regarding the latter, the

Protestant doctrine of "faith alone" was repudiated in favor of an understanding of justification in which one is accepted by God on the basis of internal righteousness, infused into one's soul through the sacraments.[12] In both instances—authority and salvation—you'll notice the centrality of the Roman Church institution as a tangible mediator between God and man. This emphasis, as we shall see, is fundamental to Catholic teaching.

The momentum of reform initiated at Trent continued after the council concluded. The work of Pius V (pontificate 1566–1572) is a prime example. An ascetic by nature who spent long hours in prayer, Pius V was equally industrious. He published the *Catechism* of the Council of Trent, an authoritative overview of the beliefs and practices of the Church, and the *Revised Roman Missal*, which provided a uniform liturgy to the universal Church. He is also credited with purging the curial bureaucracy of much of its corruption. This trajectory was continued by Pius's successor, Gregory XIII (pontificate 1572–1585).

While reform-minded popes were implementing new initiatives at the top, significant movement of renewal continued to unfold on the ground. An illustration of this movement was the Society of Jesus (commonly known as the Jesuits). Ignatius Loyola founded the Jesuits in 1534 by assembling a band of men who shared his commitment to Catholic renewal. The Society was officially recognized by Pope Paul III in 1540. The Jesuits pledged to serve God by serving the pope, which they did with great energy and effectiveness. They preached sermons, debated Protestants, founded colleges, constructed churches, wrote monographs, and traversed continents as missionaries. By the time Ignatius breathed his last in 1556, the order had over 930 members serving throughout Europe and beyond. The religious zeal that these men carried in their hearts and promoted in their work was consonant with the ethos of the Council of Trent, as one Catholic historian has noted:

> [The Council of Trent's] spirituality was then sacramental, centered on the Eucharist. It was exacting, making stiff demands on its practitioners: self-discipline, self-control, and regularity in prayer. It was practical in the way it closely associated good works with self-improvement. And finally, in accordance with the dominant cultural trend of the times, it was humanistic — at least in its assumption that each person had it in his power, to some degree, to determine his own fate.[13]

IDEOLOGIES CLASH

With the growth of Catholic influence, particularly in the lands of Germany, the so-called Peace of Augsburg (1555) collapsed and gave way to a disgraceful event in the history of the church: the Thirty Years' War (1618–1648). During this period, Catholics and Protestants engaged one another on the field of battle to settle their differences. The military advantage fluctuated until the Treaty of Westphalia (1648) ended the conflict by providing a legal status to Catholics, Lutherans, and Calvinists in Germany. Among its many effects was the indelible demarcation of allegiance between European nations, with much of the north (England, Sweden, Switzerland, Prussia) moving toward Protestantism and the south (France, Italy, Spain) remaining Roman Catholic. The unity of medieval Christianity was now permanently gone.

In the decades leading into the eighteenth century, during the so-called Age of Reason, the Roman Catholic Church often clashed with modern thought. For example, as Kepler, Galileo, and Newton revolutionized our understanding of the cosmos, Catholic authorities responded by asserting a traditional (Aristotelian) conception of the universe. The trial of Galileo in 1633 is perhaps the most vivid illustration of this confrontation. As is well known, the church condemned Galileo's proposal of "heliocentrism" (that the earth moves around the sun). Other Enlightenment thinkers, such as René Descartes (1596–1650), found a similar reception. Some applied Descartes's principle of methodical doubting to the broader Christian tradition. This approach, whether in the writings of Voltaire or in more practical examples, such as Thomas Jefferson scissoring out miracle narratives from his Bible while sitting on the White House floor, threatened the Church's claim to speak on behalf of God.[14]

In the year 1789, when the French Revolution began, the Roman Catholic Church still exercised influence over much of Western Europe. From the perspective of most Catholics, it appeared that life was proceeding normally. However, the traditional order would soon be upset.

Like most revolutions, the Enlightenment era was birthed in the realm of ideas and words, but it wasn't long before intellectual reflection turned to action. On July 14, 1789, when a French mob stormed the Bastille (a Parisian fortress which functioned as a prison), the movement was underway. In the 1790s a revolutionary group called the National Assembly endeavored to reform the Church in France. However, when the Assembly undercut control of the pope and required Church officeholders to do the same, the Church divided down the middle. Clergy in virtually every town and village throughout the country locked horns. Eventually, the revolutionary leaders drove over thirty thousand priests from their native towns into hiding.[15]

With each passing year, revolutionary fervor grew, especially in France. After Louis XVI let in a foreign invasion to address his radicals, rioting peasants showed him the door. Actually they sent him and his family to the guillotine. As heads were rolling, the new parliament abolished Christianity in exchange for the humanist ideology of Voltaire and Rousseau. Reason was worshiped as God, the religious calendar was replaced by ten-day weeks, and saints' days became holidays celebrating fruit, vegetables, and flowers. However, in 1799, just ten years after the French Revolution started, a man arose who undermined the movement's momentum. His name was Napoleon Bonaparte.

Under Napoleon's leadership the French army conquered Italy, including the city of Rome. While not exactly a paragon of fidelity to his Church, Napoleon recognized Catholicism as a friend to his social order. Historian Stephen Tomkins describes what this "friendship" looked like:

> So Napoleon offered Pope Pius VII a deal. He would restore the church if the Pope approved his regime, but bishops would be chosen by and swear allegiance to Napoleon, and Jews and Protestants would still be tolerated. Pius agreed, but he became increasingly annoyed by Napoleon's manipulation of the church. In 1804, Napoleon induced him to come and crown him emperor in Notre Dame, repaying the favour Pope Leo had paid Charlemagne 1,000 years before, but in a pointed twist of the tale, Napoleon whipped the crown out of the Pope's hands at the last minute and crowned himself ... Finally, when Napoleon annexed the Papal State to France, Pius excommunicated him, so Napoleon arrested the Pope.[16]

By his military and political exploits, Napoleon had unwittingly taken the Revolution further than it had gone before. He not only broke the alliance of throne and altar in France, but he also carried division to Rome itself. Swiss and other mercenaries offered virtually no resistance to Napoleon's invasion of 1796. Humiliated by the French sword, Pope Pius VI (and his successor Pius VII) were divested of political power. When Napoleon's empire collapsed in 1815 and he was banished to a desolate island in the Atlantic, the Congress of Vienna restored the Papal States and placed them under Austrian protection; however, the days of her self-governing power were now gone.

A NEW REALITY

After a few years of relative peace, a movement for Italian independence and solidarity called *Risorgimento* ("rebirth") arose in Sardinia. Eager to see the Italian peninsula united under a common flag, revolutionaries considered the Papal States to be a medieval vestige which stood in the way of their dream. A host of conspiracies and revolts characterized the following decades, especially between 1831 and 1849, as political factions jockeyed for power. The pontiff found himself in the middle of this explosive politick.

At first, proponents of *Risorgimento* regarded Pope Pius IX (called "Pio Nono," pontificate 1846–1878) as an ally, but their alliance didn't last long. Historian Bruce Shelley offers a cogent summary of how things soured:

> Liberals initially welcomed Pope Pius IX. He was a warm, kindly, well-meaning man, and the liberals took him for a true reformer when, on 14 March 1848, he gave the Papal States a constitution that permitted the people a moderate degree of participation in their government. Some dreamed of an Italian federation under the pope. But Pius suddenly changed his mind about the Papal States when revolutionaries assassinated the first papal prime minister, Count Pellegrino Rossi. Revolution broke out in Rome, and Pius was forced to flee. With French military help he regained Rome and the Papal States, but this time Pius insisted to a return to the old absolutist rule.[17]

Through a series of eventful (and ironic) turns, Rome found security in the protection of French troops. But the respite was short lived. When the Franco-Prussian War drew the French military home from Italy, Rome was left unprotected. A new Italian army led by nationalists immediately attacked the Papal States, and Pope Pius IX surrendered. Following a referendum, Rome was declared Italy's capital city. When it was formally annexed on October 20, 1870, a thousand years of Papal State sovereignty came to an end. Consequently, Pius IX retreated into a self-imposed captivity in the Vatican.

We can only imagine the pope's consternation as he was forced to surrender the Papal States. While no one knows what was going through his mind, his response is a matter of history. In 1870, the same year when political rule was seized from Pope Pius IX, during the Vatican Council (in retrospect, we call it the First Vatican Council) he declared the doctrine of papal infallibility—the teaching that a pope is preserved from error when solemnly pronouncing Catholic dogma on faith and morals. Although Pius IX was stripped of his political role, he maintained a jurisdiction beyond the reach of any king or prince in the spiritual realm. In this realm there was one earthly throne and one pontiff with the authority to speak from it. As stated in the pope's decree, *Pastor Aeternus* ("Eternal Pastor"):

> Therefore, faithfully adhering to the tradition received from the beginning of the christian faith, to the glory of God our savior, for the exaltation of the Catholic religion and for the salvation of the christian people, with the approval of the Sacred Council, we teach and define as a divinely revealed dogma that when

the Roman Pontiff speaks *ex cathedra*, that is, when, in the exercise of his office as shepherd and teacher of all Christians, in virtue of his supreme apostolic authority, he defines a doctrine concerning faith or morals to be held by the whole Church, he possesses, by the divine assistance promised to him in blessed Peter, that infallibility which the divine Redeemer willed his Church to enjoy in defining doctrine concerning faith or morals. Therefore, such definitions of the Roman Pontiff are of themselves, and not by the consent of the Church, irreformable. So then, should anyone, which God forbid, have the temerity to reject this definition of ours: let him be anathema.[18]

PRISONERS OF THE VATICAN

Pope Pius IX is an important figure in papal history. Elected in 1846, he held the office for thirty-two years, longer than any other pope. He is the pope who pronounced Mary's Immaculate Conception in 1854 (the belief that Jesus' mother was conceived without original sin), and ten years later he issued the so-called Syllabus of Errors (a condemnation of modern ideas and conventions that Catholics were to avoid). Under his leadership, the popular image of the Roman Catholic Church led by an authoritative pope in a defensive posture against the modern world was solidified, an image that extended into the twentieth century. Concerning the influence of this legacy on future generations, Roman Catholic journalist and commentator David Gibson provides a portrait:

In a 1906 encyclical, Pius X said that the "one duty" of the laity "is to allow themselves to be led, and like a docile flock, to follow the Pastors." In 1907 the American hierarchy followed suit with a similar directive: "The Church is not a republic or a democracy, but a monarchy; ... all her authority is from above and rests in her Hierarchy ... [While] the faithful of the laity have divinely given rights to receive all the blessed ministrations of the Church, they have absolutely no right whatever to rule and govern."[19]

When Pius IX died, he was succeeded by another outstanding pope, Leo XIII. While also a virtual prisoner of the Vatican for the duration of his pontificate (1879 – 1903), Leo shaped Catholicism in significant ways. He is sometimes recognized as the founder of the modern papacy and the one responsible for spiritual renewal that extends to the present.[20] An example of this renewal is found in Leo's encyclical letter, *Annum Sacrum* (promulgated on May 25, 1899), in which he decreed the consecration of the entire human race to the Sacred Heart of Jesus, a movement that emphasized the need for personal devotion in the face of an increasingly aggressive advance of secularism. According to Leo, friendship with Jesus Christ, the merciful Shepherd, is necessarily a central feature of Catholic Christianity.

Although Leo XIII was also a conservative, he had broader horizons than his predecessor. One expression of his inquisitive character was his practice of studying Church history in search of devotional practices that could serve the contemporary Church. From his reading of the Middle Ages, Leo acquired particular interest in encouraging the use of the rosary.[21] Similarly, Leo became fond of certain Scholastic theologians, most significantly Thomas Aquinas (1225 – 1274). Under Leo's leadership, the writings of Aquinas, especially the *Summa Theologica*, reached new heights. Henceforth, candidates for the priesthood would read Aquinas as an essential part of their seminary training.

Perhaps the most famous aspect of Leo's legacy is his encyclical, *Rerum Novarum* (1891, literally "New Things," properly titled "Rights and Duties of Capital and Labor"). Called the Magna Carta of Catholic social teaching (first by Pius XI forty years later and then by historians ever since), its significance is hard to overestimate. We must remember that Leo's pontificate coincided with the industrial revolution, a period of terrible agony for large portions of the European population. Those who have read *Oliver Twist* by Charles Dickens, for example, will recall the bitter pain and misery of factory workers, including women and children, who were exploited and oppressed for the economic benefit of industrial barons. In the face of such injustice, Leo spoke on behalf of laborers, calling business owners to address the "misery and wretchedness pressing so unjustly on the majority of the working class."[22] *Rerum Novarum* develops basic concepts of social thought, such as the dignity of human persons and the need to pursue the common good. And in very practical terms, Leo called for regulation of work hours, better working conditions, and the need for rest. In Leo's words:

Therefore, those whom fortune favors are warned that riches do not bring freedom from sorrow and are of no avail for eternal happiness, but rather are obstacles; that the rich should tremble at the threatenings of Jesus Christ — threatenings so unwonted in the mouth of our Lord and that a most strict account must be given to the Supreme Judge for all we possess.[23]

Leo's vision for a democratic political community, a free economy, and a robust moral culture effectively challenged Catholics to engage the struggle for social justice, and it continues to do so today. Indeed, a connection is commonly drawn between contemporary Catholic values for social reform and the fundamental principles outlined in *Rerum Novarum*. Such commitments include the dignity of human persons (embodied, for example, in opposition to abortion, euthanasia, and the death penalty), a call to family and community participation, fundamental rights, care for the poor and vulnerable, dignity of work and rights of workers, peaceful solidarity between nations, and the care of creation.[24] John Paul II's Encyclical Letter commemorating the hundredth anniversary of *Rerum Novarum*, *Centesimus Annus* (1991), is one of many examples of the ongoing significance of these values.

END OF AN ERA

Leo's successor, Pius X (pontificate 1903 – 1914) came from a relatively poor Italian family. Known primarily as a gifted pastor, Pius insisted that laypeople should receive communion often. We should remember that since the Fourth Lateran Council in the year 1215 it was mandatory for Catholics to receive communion once a year. In practice, however, many if not most Catholics took communion *only* once a year (some would have received it two or three times a year, but rarely more). Building on Leo's emphasis on lay piety, Pius promoted communal worship by inviting the faithful to partake of communion often, even daily. Pius X was deeply loved by Catholics on account of his personal piety. In just a few decades he was canonized.

Following the brief pontificate of Benedict XV (1914–1922), Pius XI was crowned as pope (1922–1939). His most notable achievement was an agreement with the Italian government which finally addressed the political status of the papacy. In the Lateran Treaty signed in 1929, Pius XI officially surrendered all claims to the Papal States. In return, the pope was given sovereignty over the Vatican, a few acres in the city of Rome surrounding Saint Peter's Basilica. Pius also issued a decree on the fortieth anniversary of *Rerum Novarum* (called *Quadragesimo Anno*, "The Fortieth Year") making application of Leo's principles to his own day, which included the struggles and strains of the Great Depression.

The next pope, Pius XII (1939–1958), has gone down in history as among the more controversial occupants of Peter's chair. Having served the Church as a widely traveled diplomat (he was the first Cardinal to visit the United States who later became pope), Pius XII ruled during the turbulent years of World War II. On the favorable side, he is remembered as the pope who constructed amicable bridges to the modern world. For example, he did not forbid discussion of the theory of evolution, and he encouraged biblical scholarship and reading of Scripture by laypeople. He also decreed the first infallible statement since the dogma of infallibility was established in 1870, the Assumption of the Virgin Mary (1950, the notion that Mary's body and soul were assumed into heaven). On the controversial side, however, Pius XII has been criticized for failing to sufficiently use his authority to help the Jews during the Holocaust. Many have defended Pius, convincingly I think, pointing out that the pope did more to help the Jewish people than is generally recognized. He explicitly condemned anti-Semitism and hid Jews in the Vatican. Many critics, however, are not convinced. A small library of books containing sensational stories of conspiracy theories exists on the subject.

Sometimes historians describe the period from the French Revolution until the death of Pius XII in 1958 as the "long nineteenth century." It was an era marked by a definite conservatism among Roman Catholic popes and by most of the Church-at-large. With the next pope, however, this period drew to a close. Cardinal Angelo Roncalli of Venice (1881 – 1963) was from a humble background. Similar to Pius X, he was widely regarded as a "pastor's pastor," a lover of people. After his election to the papacy on October 28, 1958, at the ripe age of seventy-seven, he took the name John XXIII (based partly upon his reading of John's gospel, chapter 10). On that same day he summarized the personal aims of his pontificate in terms of emulating Jesus, the Good Shepherd. Few people would have suspected that this warm old man in the twilight of life would be responsible for calling one of the most significant councils in the history of the church: Vatican II.[25]

A NEW DAY DAWNS

Pope John XXIII (pontificate 1958–1963) enjoyed making new friends and was especially sympathetic to the marginalized and suffering. He often ventured out to visit orphanages and jails, and when a group of Jews once visited him, he embraced them with the biblical greeting, "I am Joseph, your brother."[26] He even granted a papal audience to a traveling circus and fondly patted a lion cub named Dolly.[27] The world would soon learn that this pontiff was not only calm among lions, but he was also impervious to the roar of modernity which had sent many of his earlier predecessors running defensively into the Vatican fortress.

Instead of the citadel image of the Roman Church that was forged during the age of Pius IX, Vatican II portrayed the Church as a "Pilgrim People" on the move throughout the modern world.[28] Toward this end, the council was designed to pursue "pastoral" aims (unlike Trent and Vatican I, which focused mainly on doctrinal reform).[29] The particular term used by John XXIII for this pursuit was *aggiornamento*, an Italian word meaning "bringing up to date." Among its chief concerns was the relationship between the authority of the pope and his bishops, and how such authority finds expression in the modern world.

From 1959 to 1962 the pope invited suggestions from bishops. He established commissions to prepare agendas and compose drafts of discussion documents. Finally, on Thursday, October 11, 1962, Vatican II started with a continuous procession of bishops in miters and flowing vestments entering St. Peter's Basilica. After the 2,400 Council Fathers were in place, the portable throne of Pope John XXIII was lowered at the entrance whereupon the pontiff proceeded to walk down the 624-foot aisle amidst clerical cheers and applause. Pope John XXIII expressed hope that if he were not still alive by the council's end, he would have the privilege of watching its conclusion from heaven. This statement turned out to be more prophetic than anyone realized at the time. On June 3, 1963, after completing the first of four sessions, Pope John XXIII died.

The general sessions of Vatican II were held at St. Peter's Basilica in the autumns of four successive years from 1962 through 1965. The primary participants were of course Catholic bishops, nearly three thousand of whom were in attendance at any one time. For those whose hearts desired it, a sense of renewal was in the air. John XXIII established this ethos in statements such as his exhortation from Matthew 16, in which he urged his brothers to carefully consider "signs of the times." This impulse, buttressed by movements such as the New Theology (*La Nouvelle Théologie*) made the prospects of Church renewal exciting. For some, however—particularly older members of the Roman Curia (the Vatican's senior level governing body)—the prospect of such change felt threatening. Given the lively debate that characterized session one, some questioned whether the council would resume. But it did. Pope Paul VI (pontificate 1963–1978), the successor of John XXIII, convened the second session on September 29, 1963.

I won't indulge in a close examination of the Vatican II story, though it is well worth telling. Our main concern here is to consider how the distinctive threads of church authority which we have been tracing thus far were woven together. In order to gain perspective on the tapestry's finished form, I will consider a couple of anecdotes. The first occurred during the council; the second happened just after it.

Generally speaking, there were two extremes represented at the council. "Some Catholic conservatives hoped to reassert the kind of top-down papal supremacy that had characterized the decrees of the First Vatican Council (1869–70)."[30] The Roman Curia championed this position. "[On the other side of the spectrum were those who] wanted the church to embrace progressive movements of social renewal and theological modernism."[31] The clash of these factions produced more than a few sparks.

The question of whether it was appropriate for the Mass to be spoken in the vernacular instead of Latin provoked an especially fierce debate. An outspoken voice was Archbishop Enrico Dante, who served as the

Secretary of the Sacred Congregation. As a Curia member (and outstanding Latinist) he insisted that "Latin should continue to be the language of the liturgy, and the vernacular should be used only for instructions and certain prayers."[32]

The liturgy debate continued for quite some time. Eventually, the most powerful Curia member of all, Cardinal Alfredo Ottaviani, took the podium to exhort progressives on how they should consider the Mass. The story is told by Catholic historian Rev. Dr. Ralph M. Wiltgen:

> On October 30, the day after his seventy-second birthday, Cardinal Ottaviani addressed the council to protest against the drastic changes which were being suggested in the Mass. "Are we seeking to stir up wonder, or perhaps scandal, among the Christian people, by introducing changes in so venerable a rite, that has been approved for so many centuries and is now so familiar? The rite of Holy Mass should not be treated as if it were a piece of cloth to be refashioned according to the whim of each generation." Speaking without a text, because of his partial blindness, he exceeded the ten-minute time limit which all had been requested to observe. Cardinal Tisserant, Dean of the Council Presidents, showed his watch to Cardinal Alfrink, who was presiding that morning. When Cardinal Ottaviani reached fifteen minutes, Cardinal Alfrink rang the warning bell. But the speaker was so engrossed in his topic that he did not notice the bell, or purposely ignored it. At a signal from Cardinal Alfrink, a technician switched off the

microphone. After confirming the fact by tapping the instrument, Cardinal Ottaviani stumbled back to his seat in humiliation. The most powerful cardinal in the Roman Curia had been silenced, and the Council Fathers clapped with glee.[33]

The above anecdote epitomizes the daring spirit of Vatican II and is one of many examples of how the tide was turning during the council. Contrary to the fortress mentality, the Catholic Church reached out to the world in fresh ways. For instance, ecumenical bridges were built to Eastern Orthodoxy and Judaism. Protestants, who were previously considered to be heretics (since the Council of Trent), were elevated to the more favorable plane of "separated brethren." Some of them were even invited to observe the council. The wedge between tradition and Scripture (as many scholars understand it) was removed.[34] A decree on the freedom of religion was declared. Papal authority was diffused as the role of bishops was increased. Bible study was further encouraged for lay Catholics along with greater emphasis on personal faith.

YOU SAY YOU WANT A REVOLUTION?

The decade following Vatican II was among the most turbulent in the history of modern Catholicism. With authoritarian structures diminished and democratic reforms on the rise, innovation was natural. Shelley describes these years saying, "So many spiritual and religious landmarks were suddenly swept away that the average Catholic was left in a state of complete bewilderment."[35] This bewilderment is examined by the late Prof. Ralph M. McInerny of Notre Dame in his book titled *What Went Wrong with Vatican II*. He offers an analysis of the political inferno that was ignited in 1968 when Pope Paul VI issued his encyclical *Humanae Vitae*, the decree that condemned the use of artificial methods of contraception.[36] During the days after the pope's announcement, a significant controversy ensued.[37] McInerny writes:

> Throughout July 29, the very day Pope Paul VI's encyclical was made public, it became clear that *Humanae Vitae* was encountering massive clerical resistance. It was being treated with scorn and contempt everywhere. Long before they could have read the encyclical, Catholic theologians, sociologists, and journalists were dissociating themselves from its reported teaching. Said Fr. Robert Johann, S.J., to the *New York Times*, "The hope, I think, is that educated Catholics will ignore this document."[38]
>
> Father Charles Curran, associate professor of theology at the Catholic University of America and vice president of the American Theological Society, spearheaded an effort to solicit signatures for a statement to be published about the encyclical. When the statement was first issued, there were eighty-seven signatures. The number of those wishing to associate themselves with Father Curran's refusal to accept *Humanae Vitae* was to swell in subsequent days to more than two hundred.[39]

The two hundred signatures were published in the *New York Times* on July 30, 1968, below several of Fr. Curran's protests. Following are a few of his statements:

> It is common teaching in the Church that Catholics may dissent from authoritative, non-infallible teachings of the Magisterium, when sufficient reasons for doing so exits.[40]
>
> Therefore, as Roman Catholic theologians, conscious of our duty and our limitations, we conclude that spouses may responsibly decide according to their *conscience* that artificial contraception in some circumstances is permissible and indeed necessary to preserve and foster the values and sacredness of marriage (emphasis added).[41]
>
> It is our conviction also that true commitment to the mystery of Christ and the Church requires a candid statement of mind at this time by all Catholic theologians.[42]

After citing Fr. Curran's article in his book, McInerny offers a summary of its significance. This is the punch line:

> And yet, despite its haste and Olympian condescension, this statement makes clear that the actual content of *Humanae Vitae* was of secondary importance to the signers of the statement. Their true target was the papacy; the real burden of their remarks had to do with the locus of authority in the Church, indeed with the very nature of the Church.[43]

McInerny's conclusion is incisive. Although birth control was a massive issue, it pointed to the larger theological question of how Catholic authority operated in the Church. That is, to what extent can the pope establish doctrine, and how binding are such edicts upon the consciences of individual believers?

"BE NOT AFRAID"

When Paul VI died, the Cardinals gathered in conclave and surprised the world by choosing the little known Patriarch of Venice, Albino Luciani, who selected the name John Paul I (1978). With the first double name in papal history, John Paul assumed the names of his two predecessors (John XXIII and Paul VI), suggesting that he intended to perpetuate the Vatican II legacy. His upbeat and approachable personality made him well liked, but thirty-three days after his coronation he was dead.

If the world was surprised by the choice of John Paul I, the Cardinals' decision on his successor was even more shocking. Cardinal Karol Józef Wojtyla of Poland was the first non-Italian pope to be elected in 456 years. For his papal name, Wojtyla chose John Paul II, by which he also drew continuity with the recent past. He was young, just 58 years old. An athlete, playwright, holder of two doctorates, this polymath of a man would break much of the papal mold, an act that he would continue to perform over the next 27 years (1978–2005).

How can John Paul II's legacy possibly be summarized? During his long and active pontificate, which included visits to 129 countries, he opposed fascism, communism, materialism, abortion, relativism, unbridled capitalism, divorce, and the so-called culture of death. He appointed thousands of bishops; he was the first pope since the early centuries of the church to visit a Jewish synagogue; and he presided over the publication of the *Catechism of the Catholic Church*. He is often credited with contributing to the collapse of communism in Central and Eastern Europe while at the same time lifting up young people by initiating World Youth Day (in 1984). According to George Weigel, John Paul II's most enduring theological contribution is his "theology of the body."[44] Perhaps the most vivid memory of onlookers, Catholic or otherwise, is the courageous manner in which Pope John II faced death. Despite two assassination attempts (one in which he was critically wounded), Parkinson's disease, a broken leg, hearing loss, and severe osteoarthritis—all of which debilitated his health to the point of profound physical suffering—he continued to travel the world and appear in public. In this way, John Paul II not only embodied his faith with dignity and courage, but he challenged the world to do the same.

In many respects, John Paul II defies the categories commonly used to evaluate popes. Was he a traditionalist or a progressive? To some extent, the answer is "yes" to both. In support of the latter, he castigated the excesses of unchecked capitalism and advocated on behalf of the poor. He also stood against war and violence. He decried the attacks on the World Trade Center and opposed the war in Iraq. He went so far as to apologize for acts of violence that had been conducted by the Church over the centuries, such as the Crusades, the sacking of Constantinople (1204), and the burning of John Hus (1415). He was the first pope to visit a mosque, and even kissed the Koran.

John Paul II was also quite traditional. He opposed artificial birth control, abortion, euthanasia, and homosexual practices. He reasserted the need for clerical celibacy and staunchly opposed the notion of ordaining women to the priesthood. He sought to eliminate the influence of liberation theology (often working through the Congregation for the Doctrine of the Faith, led by Joseph Cardinal Ratzinger), and he canonized more saints than any other pope in history. He was also deeply devoted to the Virgin Mary, famously putting an "M" on his papal crest, with a special devotion to Our Lady of Fatima. Thus, in view of the competing legacies of Vatican II, one finds John Paul II reflecting both impulses: progressive and traditional. Perhaps this is a reason why the late pontiff has moved so quickly toward his own canonization with the title "John Paul the Great."

THE NEW EVANGELIZATION

It is not uncommon to hear Catholics lauding Pope John Paul II, followed by relative disappointment in his successor, Benedict XVI (pontificate 2005–2013). It fell to Benedict to preside over the Church during a period of scandal, the revelation of sexual abuse perpetrated by priests. The scholarly, severe, and strongly conservative Benedict, in the eyes of these Catholics at least, is often viewed as narrower and less congenial by comparison. Ironically, however, among evangelical Protestants, it tends to be the other way around. John Paul, for all of his strengths, is often regarded with suspicion and sometimes contempt by Evangelicals because of his intense devotion to Mary and apparent endorsement of non-Christian religions (such as in his World Day of Prayer). Benedict, on the other hand, has been called the greatest biblical theologian to serve as pope. He was fond of quoting Jerome: "Ignorance of the Scriptures is ignorance of Christ." This emphasis has led many Protestants to read his books and resonate with his biblical focus.

The suggestion that Pope Benedict conveyed evangelical values might seem curious to some, especially given the traditional orientation for which he was labeled "God's Rottweiler" during his years as Cardinal-Prefect of the Congregation for the Doctrine of the Faith. In this period, for instance, he wrote *Dominus Iesus* (2000), which asserts that Protestants "are not churches in the proper sense" and that "they suffer from defects." But the manner in which the pope addressed biblical truth to the contemporary pantheon of idols, pointing out where liberty had become license and theology had been reduced to hollow sentiment, garnered a considerable amount of support among Evangelicals. However, concerning the centrality of the Bible, Benedict denounced the Reformation principle of *sola scriptura* ("Scripture alone"), suggesting that it is responsible for spawning theological liberalism and present-day relativism.

Pope Benedict surprised the world on February

11, 2013 when he announced his resignation from the papacy, a move that hadn't been made (by a pope's own volition) since Celestine V relinquished the office in 1294. The stated reason for Benedict's decision was his declining health due to old age. The Cardinals entered conclave to choose a successor and emerged with the name Jorge Mario Bergoglio, Archbishop of Buenos Aires, Argentina, who took the name of Francis. Even though we are only a little more than a year into Francis's pontificate at the time of this writing, the new pope has received enormous media attention. For example, news headlines are currently full of reports on *America Magazine*'s recent interview. You will perhaps recall the interviewer's first question, "Who is Jorge Mario Bergoglio?" to which the pope responded, "I am a sinner. This is the most accurate definition. It is not a figure of speech, a literary genre. I am a sinner."

The pope's focus on sin and personal repentance strikes a chord among Evangelicals, as does his stress on the need for mercy. Emerging from his motto — *miserando atque eligando* ("by making mercy and choosing [to practice it]," also sometimes translated "lowly but chosen") — is a discernible theme that appears to run through the whole of Bergoglio's ministry. Once again, evangelical Protestants will find this emphasis refreshing. At the same time, however, there are dimensions of Francis's ministry that Evangelicals find troubling, such as his deep Marian devotion (in his first speech as pope he committed himself and the world to Mary) and his comments about Christian salvation extending to atheists who sincerely obey their consciences. For better or for worse, Francis is generating a great deal of conversation.

TODAY'S ROMAN CATHOLIC CHURCH

Looking back over the last five hundred years of Catholic Church history, we have observed numerous developments. Not unlike St. Peter's Basilica itself, which has grown layer by layer—a burial site where Christians gathered to pray, an original Basilica, followed by a new, spectacular building—Catholic tradition has gradually developed into its current form. This chapter has noted how the accumulation of these beliefs and conventions has taken shape, including the impulse for reform, renewed intellectual and cultural heritage, articulation of papal authority, robust moral theology, liturgical reform, *aggiornamento*, theology of the body, empowerment of youth, and biblical theology. The aggregate of these movements (and many more) is the tradition of the Roman Catholic Church.

Hopefully this overview will enable you to recognize why Catholics do many of the things they do. We have noted that devotional practices such as the rosary and prayer to the Sacred Heart of Jesus were popularized by Leo XIII to deepen piety in the face of growing secularism. We also observed how the same pope fortified the Church's commitment to serving and protecting the poor through initiatives of social justice. We've seen how the birth control debate ignited an inferno of controversy and how it revealed an even bigger disagreement concerning the extent to which Church authority can speak into the personal affairs of Catholic men and women. In light of these observations, it is fascinating to consider how circumstances have changed and in other respects have remained remarkably similar. King Solomon's statement about there being "nothing new under the sun" rings true.

If you are like me, you read this historical overview as an evangelical Protestant and you are conflicted. Recognizing expressions of truth that emerge from the Bible and honor Christ, we want to cheer for their advance. And yet there are elements of Catholic tradition that not only fall short of the Bible but seemingly clash with it. So significant are these differences that they extend to the gospel message itself, complicating and confusing the faith with which one believes in Christ and is saved. How then can evangelical Protestants fairly and judiciously understand the Roman Catholic Church, that is, in a way that upholds grace and truth? This is the subject of our next two chapters.

CHAPTER FOUR

SIMILARITIES AND DIFFERENCES BETWEEN CATHOLICS AND PROTESTANTS

Much common ground exists between orthodox Roman Catholics and evangelical Protestants, a fact that we often overlook. For instance, we both seek to build our faith upon the Bible.[1] We agree on basic doctrines such as the Trinity, the person and mission of Jesus Christ, and the plight of humanity.[2] We embrace the Apostles' and Nicene Creeds. We admire many of the same figures from church history; cherish many of the same literary works, such as Augustine's *Confessions*, Thomas à Kempis's *The Imitation of Christ*, and J. R. R. Tolkien's *The Lord of the Rings*. We also stand together at the corner of moral conviction and public virtue—advocating on behalf of religious freedom, the poor, a free market economy, the preservation of life, and a biblical definition of marriage. These commonalities are important and should be acknowledged.

But we also have differences. The sufficiency and authority of Scripture remains a fundamental issue of disagreement. In addition to the text of Scripture, Catholicism builds her faith with the resources of Sacred Tradition and Magisterium (the teaching office of the Church).[3] We disagree on the office and authority of the pope. Protestants believe that the Church's supreme authority is the Bible. Finally, and perhaps most significantly, we disagree on how exactly one is saved. Catholics understand the inner workings of God's grace to occur through the sacraments in a *process* of justification whereby the gift of righteousness is "infused" into one's soul.[4] Protestants believe that justification is fundamentally based on the crediting of Christ's righteousness, accessed by faith alone. Following from these differences are a host of others, such as the perpetual sacrifice of the Mass, purgatory, indulgences, veneration of the Saints, penance, and the mediating role of Mary.

This chapter seeks to offer perspective on the basic differences between Catholic and Protestant belief. I'll begin with a little illustration.[5] Many years ago, I worked as a professional fundraiser in the Catholic Church. One evening, at a black-tie affair on Palm Beach Island, I was presenting our appeal to a large group of wealthy donors. Before the bishop opened in prayer, our team reviewed the agenda one last time. We then discovered our mistake. All the campaign elements were in place—volunteers, video, brochures; the issue was the food. On the menu was an entrée of filet mignon, twice-baked potato, and vegetable. At any other time of the year, steak would have been great; unfortunately, this particular Friday was during Lent, a special religious season when Catholics abstain from eating meat. To consume meat on a Friday during Lent constitutes a sin. If one should die after doing so, it would put them into the flames of purgatory (or perhaps worse). This was a serious problem!

In actual practice, many Catholics *do* eat meat on Fridays during Lent, but they don't usually do it when dining with the bishop and clergy. Further, it is unthinkable that the Catholic Church would serve such a meal. The salad and a dinner roll would buy us about twenty minutes. The Lord's multiplying of fish crossed my mind more than once.

While our team of fundraisers nervously looked at one another in silent bewilderment, the bishop initiated our conversation. He reiterated what we already knew concerning Lenten food laws and the implications for our predicament. He continued, "As the bishop, I have the authority to declare a special dispensation which will allow us to eat meat during Lent. If there is ever a time for such a provision, it is now." I then observed the bishop ascend the platform, announce the menu, and before guests connected the doctrinal dots, he pronounced a special blessing to sanction the meal. My eyes turned toward old Joe Sedlak, who sat beside me thinking that if he had choked on his steak and died apart from the bishop's blessing, he would have been roasted. But now, after the bishop's prayer, he could feast in peace.

From an evangelical Protestant point of view, clerical authority of this kind is inexplicable. Because salvation comes by believing in Jesus who died for our sins and rose for our justification, such activity doesn't make sense to Protestants. Yet the bishop's announcement fit comfortably within the context of Catholic thought. If authority is vested in the bishops to the extent that they mediate the forgiveness and sanctifying grace of Christ, then such clerical activity follows logically.

Later, I grasped that Church authority is the fulcrum that distinguishes Catholics from Protestants. Is authority located in the bishops by means of apostolic succession? If you say yes, you will resonate with Roman Catholicism. If instead you find supreme authority to be in Scripture alone, you are an evangelical Protestant. In what follows, we will consider these two approaches. Because this chapter is the most doctrinal in the book, you may benefit from reading some portions more slowly.

Sometimes, when I am teaching on the authority structure of Catholicism, I show the introduction to Fr. Robert Barron's DVD series, *Catholicism*. I ask the class to note the visible elements of Catholic authority, especially those that reflect the person and work of Christ. In addition to the elevated Bible, chalice, and Roman statue of the apostle Peter, students will sometimes ask me about a favorite phrase of Fr. Barron's: "grounded in Christ." A key to its meaning is found in the various images that viewers observe when Fr. Barron uses the phrase. They are symbols depicting the institution of the Church (e.g., candles, statues, priests in procession, a bishop, the Mass). Why is this significant? As anyone familiar with Catholic doctrine understands, the way for humanity to be "grounded" in Christ, that is, to encounter his saving presence, is to be in communion with the Roman Catholic Church. Here is how it works.

OUR FUNDAMENTAL DIFFERENCE

A few statements from the *Catechism of the Catholic Church* will get us started. Notice the connection between the person of Jesus Christ and the institution of the Roman Catholic Church:

> The Church is both visible and spiritual, a hierarchical society and the *Mystical Body of Christ.* She is one, yet formed of two components, human and divine. That is her mystery, which only faith can accept.[6]
>
> The Church in this world is the sacrament of salvation, the sign and the instrument of the communion of God and men.[7]

The reason why the Catholic Church regards herself as the "Mystical Body of Christ" is often summarized by the word "incarnation."[8] Most of us have heard the term during Advent and Christmas. The incarnation describes the historical event in which the second person of the triune God became a man. On this Catholics and Evangelicals agree — born of a virgin, Jesus of Nazareth is fully God and fully man. In Catholic thought, however, "incarnation" has a broader and deeper meaning, as it also describes the embodiment of Jesus *in the institution of the Roman Catholic Church*. Consider, for instance, the following statement from Pope Emeritus Benedict XVI.

> The notion of the body of Christ was developed in the Catholic Church to the effect that the Church designated as "Christ living on earth" came to mean that the Church was described as the Incarnation of the Son continuing until the end of time.[9]

How does one encounter the life and salvation of Jesus, according to Catholic teaching? It is in communion with the Roman Catholic Church, that is, "Christ living on earth." It must be pointed out that evangelical Protestants also recognize a vital union (often described as "spiritual" or "mystical") between Christ and his Church.[10] Because the Holy Spirit lives within God's people, the Church is a supernatural society with divine and human dimensions. The Catholic position, however, is far more indebted to the logic of incarnation. In the words of the late Fr. Richard John Neuhaus, "For the Catholic, faith in Christ and faith in the Church are one act of faith."[11] In this statement, Neuhaus is simply echoing the words of the *Catechism*: "Christ and his Church thus together make up the 'whole Christ.' "[12] In this way, "incarnation" is not simply a historical event from two millennia ago; it is the ongoing bond that makes the Church a single subject with Christ.[13]

If, as the Catholic Church asserts, she is Christ living on earth, in what ways does she exercise Christ's authority? In addition to basing her beliefs on Scripture, the Church also builds its faith with the resources of "Sacred Tradition." This is the second of three elements of Catholic authority. Such Tradition is viewed as the "Word of God" along with the Bible itself, which is to say that when Catholics speak of "God's Word," they have in mind Scripture *and* Tradition. In the words of the *Catechism*:

> Sacred Tradition and Sacred Scripture make up a single sacred deposit of the "Word of God" (*DV* 10), in which, as in a mirror, the pilgrim Church contemplates God, the source of all her riches.[14]

A helpful illustration of how Sacred Tradition comes into being is found in the doctrine of Mary's Assumption (the belief that Mary's body and soul were assumed into heaven), which was established on November 1, 1950, by Pope Pius XII. The formal process started in 1946 when Pius sent a letter to the bishops of the world, inviting their opinion on whether the Assumption should be made a dogma of the Roman Catholic faith. He asked two questions: "Do you, venerable brethren, in your outstanding wisdom and prudence, judge that the bodily Assumption of the Blessed Virgin can be proposed and defined as a dogma of faith? Do you, with your clergy and people, desire it?"[15] The pope's question sent the bishops of the Church to investigate whether Mary's Assumption could be found in the two sources of Catholic revelation: Scripture and Tradition. Since there is no mention of Mary's death, burial, or assumption in Scripture, attention quickly turned to Tradition.

An examination of Tradition required bishops to review the faith and practice of popes, other bishops, and laypeople through the centuries. With these groups in view, attention was then focused on seven areas: dogmatic decrees, Church creeds, Church Fathers, Church Doctors (an honorific title given to a few outstanding teachers since the early church), the teaching of bishops, universal practices of the Church, and common beliefs and piety of the faithful. After analyzing each of these areas, the bishops responded with the following conclusion. In the pope's words, "those whom 'the Holy Spirit has placed as bishops to rule the Church of God' gave an almost unanimous affirmative response."[16]

On account of their authority (remember the concept of continuous incarnation), the bishops found support for Mary's Assumption in Catholic tradition, and, on this basis, they affirmed its legitimacy. So authoritative was this affirmation that the pope described it as "entirely certain and infallible."[17] As such, the Assumption of Mary became an essential tenet of Catholic belief, a dogma commanding submission among Catholics everywhere. To disbelieve or contradict the doctrine is to commit a mortal sin, which, strictly speaking, jeopardizes one's salvation.

Needless to say, the Catholic process of establishing doctrine is quite different from the Protestant method. Even so, there is something that Protestants commonly practice when we interpret the Bible that may help us to understand the logic of the Catholic approach. When Protestants read the Old Testament, we frequently find allusions to Christ that grow into explicit references in the New Testament. Examples include Genesis 3:15 (the seed of the woman will crush the head of the serpent), Deuteronomy 18 ("God will raise up for you a prophet like [Moses]"), and Isaiah 53 (the "Suffering Servant"). The Hebrew Scriptures outline these promises before the New Testament portrays the details of their fulfillment in the second person of the triune God, Jesus Christ. Augustine famously summarized this pattern when he said (if I may paraphrase) that the Old Testament is the New concealed and the New Testament is the Old revealed.[18]

So how does this relate to the development of Catholic doctrine in her Sacred Tradition? As Protestants look to the New Testament for clarity and definition of the seminal ideas that grow out of the Old Testament, Catholics rely on the teaching and practices of Church history for authoritative definition of ideas that they find in the Bible. Over time, century by century, the church recognizes that these ideas grow and develop, taking shape into specific formulations of doctrine. These developments of doctrine are what the Catholic Church calls "Sacred Tradition."

This explanation is not intended to defend the Catholic practice but simply to illustrate how it works. From a Protestant point of view, given our commitment to "Scripture alone" as God's word, the practice of establishing dogma on the basis of Church tradition is misguided. Martin Luther made this point at the Diet of Worms (1521): "I put not trust in the unsupported authority of the pope or councils, since it is plain that they have often erred and often contradict themselves — I consider myself convicted by the testimony of Holy Scripture, which is my basis; my conscience is captive to the Word of God." Contemporary Evangelicalism resonates with Luther's concern.

The third element of Catholic authority, in addition to Sacred Tradition, is the "Magisterium," the teaching office of the Church whose task is to provide an authentic interpretation of God's word.[19] The Magisterium is not an original source of revelation (such as Scripture and Tradition); it is, rather, a way of interpreting these sources so that God's people can understand their proper meaning and significance. The late Avery Cardinal Dulles explains this need by quoting Philip's question to the Ethiopian eunuch: "Do you understand what you are reading?" To which the eunuch replied "How can I, unless someone guides me?" (Acts 8:30–31 ESV).[20] Through the Magisterium, the Catholic Church seeks to provide such guidance.

Sometimes the Magisterium speaks infallibly, though not always. According to Vatican II, it "draws from the deposit of faith [Scripture and Tradition] everything that it presents as divinely revealed."[21] As a way to picture how this works, you might envision one of those familiar stools from your local diner with the round seat supported by a solid base. Imagine that this stool also has a pad to support your back. The base on which you sit is God's word (Scripture and Tradition) and the back pad is the Church's teaching office (Magisterium). Together, they provide you with support, although they are distinct. The back pad upholds you, even though, properly speaking, it is not the base. Likewise, the Magisterium, as it provides the authentic interpretation of God's word, is a real authority without actually constituting the basis of divine revelation. As Church authority, Scripture, Tradition, and Magisterium function as a unit, defining and guiding Catholic faith.

THE EVANGELICAL PROTESTANT POSITION

As already noted, evangelical Protestants agree with Catholics that a vital union exists between Christ and his Church, a union that manifests the reality of God and his transforming grace. We stand together in affirming that Jesus Christ is our head (Eph. 4:15), the firstborn (Rom. 8:29), the One into whom we are grafted (Rom. 11:17) and clothed (Gal. 3:27). We agree that Jesus speaks to and from his Church, resulting in a deeper experience of holiness and witness to the world. From a Protestant point of view, however, the Catholic concept of continuous incarnation—the notion that Christ's infallible revelation and authority subsists in the one holy catholic apostolic Church—is unsustainable from Scripture. It's not an infallible Church that God gives us; it is the infallible Word, the Bible.[22] This conviction, that Scripture is the singular body of divine revelation and therefore the supreme authority, is what Evangelicals mean by the phrase *sola scriptura* ("Scripture alone").[23]

A first step toward understanding the concept of Scripture alone is to recognize the correlation of Jesus the *living* Word (risen and seated at God's right hand) to Jesus' authoritative *written* Word (the biblical text). Think, for instance, of how John's gospel draws this connection: "In the beginning was the Word, and the Word was with God, and the Word was God."[24] Alister McGrath offers a helpful explanation:

> When the first generation of Protestants spoke of the "authority of the Bible," this was to be understood as "the authority of the risen Christ, mediated and expressed through the Bible" ... Precisely because Jesus Christ stands at the heart of the Christian faith, Protestants argue, so must the Bible. There is the most intimate interconnection between the Bible and Christ in the Protestant tradition. The Bible is the means by which Christ is displayed, proclaimed, and manifested.[25]

A summation of the doctrine of "Scripture alone" is found in The Chicago Statement on Biblical Inerrancy, crafted by more than two hundred evangelical leaders in October 1978. It begins with the following words, "The authority of Scripture is a key issue for the Christian church in this and every age. Those who profess faith in Jesus Christ as Lord and Savior are called to show the reality of their discipleship by humbly and faithfully obeying God's written Word. To stray from Scripture in faith or conduct is disloyalty to our Master. Recognition of the total truth and trustworthiness of Holy Scripture is essential to a full grasp and adequate confession of its authority."

While all nineteen articles of the Chicago Statement relate to Scripture alone in some way, article two strikes at its heart with the following words:

> **We affirm** that the Scriptures are the supreme written norm by which God binds the conscience, and that the authority of the church is subordinate to that of Scripture.
>
> **We deny** that church creeds, councils, or declarations have authority greater than or equal to the authority of the Bible.

If, as the Catholic Church teaches, the bishops are "endowed with the authority of Christ" and share in Christ's infallibility,[26] then Christian authority would be found in the hierarchy of the Church. If, however, the inspired revelation of Jesus is the written Word alone, then Scripture is the supreme authority. On this point, the Chicago Statement offers another helpful explanation:

> By authenticating each other's authority, Christ and Scripture coalesce into a single fount of authority. The biblically-interpreted Christ and the Christ-centered, Christ-proclaiming Bible are from this standpoint one. As from the face of inspiration we infer that what Scripture says, God says, so from the revealed relation between Jesus Christ and Scripture we may equally declare that what Scripture says, Christ says.[27]

When we assert the sufficiency of Scripture, we ought to make a disclaimer. Our commitment to the sacred text should never undermine our appreciation for biblically rooted traditions. Certain standards, routines, and customs may not be explicitly stated in a chapter and verse but nonetheless provide tangible forms in which to celebrate and express Christian faith. These traditions will look different depending on one's context. As long as they are faithful to Scripture, however, such conventions should be employed for the glory of God.

So what about the Catholic claim that we need a Magisterium to provide the authoritative interpretation of God's word? Augustine is helpful here. In his work, *On Christian Doctrine*, the Bishop of Hippo addresses the challenge of interpreting obscure passages of Scripture by explaining how such passages reveal our sin-darkened intelligence. What's interesting is that Augustine says nothing of a Church Magisterium as the solution to these conundrums; rather, he portrays hard sayings as purposefully arranged by God to subdue our pride and feed charity.[28] Augustine's view on this point is also the biblical portrait. Scripture lacks any example of an infallible teaching office; nor does it have a revealed interest in one. Instead, it portrays an eschatological reality in which we now see but a poor reflection as in a mirror, awaiting the day when we will see truth face to face (1 Cor. 13:12). This reality should infuse the activity of biblical interpretation with a conscious balance of grace and truth, or, in Richard Baxter's words, "unity in necessary things; liberty in doubtful things; and charity in all things." We contend for the faith (Jude v. 3) while simultaneously preserving the unity of the Spirit in the bond of peace (Eph. 4:3).

So why is Scripture alone so important to Protestants?

It is partly on account of our sensitivity to the concern of Jesus in Matthew 15:9 where the Lord warns against presenting the "commandments of men" as God's word, since such tradition obscures and undermines biblical teaching. Professor Tony Lane captures the heart of the concern when he writes "*Sola Scriptura* is the statement that the church can err."[29] From an Evangelical's point of view, this is true of Catholic doctrines such as purgatory, indulgences, and Mary's co-mediation. Among such doctrines, the most troubling of all (for Evangelicals at least) is the Catholic teaching on how men and women experience salvation.

OUR DIFFERENT UNDERSTANDING OF SALVATION

I once taught a lesson titled "Why I Believe in Purgatory" at College Church in Wheaton, Illinois, where I served on the pastoral staff.[30] If you ever want to draw large numbers of people to hear you speak and don't mind lots of emails beforehand, you might consider using it. The facial expressions of those sitting in the session were memorable. It was like the boy who looked up at Joe Jackson after the famous White Sox player was found guilty of fixing the 1919 World Series and exclaimed, "Say it ain't so, Joe." Many evidently thought that it would be my theological coming out party—true confessions of a closet Catholic. I suspect it didn't help that I started my presentation with the words, "I believe in purgatory."

TALKING WITH CATHOLICS ABOUT THE GOSPEL

Toward the end of the lesson my wife wore a facial expression that said, *Please stop keeping them in suspense.* I then realized that it was time to explain. My comments went something like this:

• • •

Some of you are wondering how your evangelical Protestant pastor can believe in purgatory. The word "purgatory" describes purification or purging from sin. In the Roman Catholic tradition, this is believed to happen after people die in order for them to enter heaven spotless and pure. On the basis of Scripture, I also believe in purgatory; however, I believe that it happened once and for all on the cross of Christ when the Lord hung between heaven and earth and shed his blood. Dying as our substitute, Jesus purged our sin. He paid the penalty for our guilt once and for all, even as it says in 1 Peter 3:18:

> For Christ also suffered once for sins, the righteous for the unrighteous, to bring you to God. He was put to death in the body but made alive in the Spirit.

In his death, Jesus perfectly satisfied the righteous demands of God's law for us. It is a gift that we cannot earn. Not even Abraham, the friend of God, could merit this favor. Therefore, Paul writes in Romans 4:2–5:

> If, in fact, Abraham was justified by works, he had something to boast about—but not before God. What does Scripture say? "Abraham believed God, and it was credited to him as righteousness." Now to the one who works, wages are not credited as a gift but as an obligation. However, to the one who does not

work but trusts God who justifies the ungodly, their faith is credited as righteousness.

Martin Luther offered a helpful illustration of this truth. One winter day he was sitting among his students when snow started to fall. Luther pointed to a pile of manure beside his home and explained that on account of sin the moral condition of humanity resembles the stinking pile of dung. Among the implications of this condition are guilt and condemnation before God.

Within the hour, snow had fallen so steadily that the dunghill was completely covered. Luther once again paused from his lesson and pointed to the mound. He asked the students what they saw. Instead of manure, the students described a lovely white, powdery hill. As the sunlight gleamed off the fresh snow, Luther stated, "That is how the Father sees us in Christ. While we remain sinful, in Christ we are clothed with his perfect righteousness, on the basis of which we are accepted." This is why Paul can say in Romans 8:1, "Therefore, there is now no condemnation for those who are in Christ Jesus."

I must hasten to point out that Luther's dung metaphor is imperfect. Because God provides his Holy Spirit and actively conforms us to Christ, we actually grow in holiness and become more than dung. This is where Luther's analogy breaks down. But there is another part of the image that is not only accurate, it is central to the gospel. It is the fact that when God looks upon us, he regards us not according to our sin, but, rather, according to the perfect righteousness of Christ. This is what makes the gospel good news.

• • •

Although my stated belief in purgatory was a (lame) attempt to pique interest and provoke thinking, it also makes a point. Catholics and Protestants agree that sin requires purging. Following Augustine, we both recognize the damning effects of human rebellion that leave us desperate for God's saving grace. Our difference consists in how we understand God to forgive our sins and accept us as his children. In theological terms, this is called the "doctrine of justification." We begin with a look at the Catholic position.

When an infant is carried to the font for the sacrament of baptism, the priest blesses and anoints the child before pouring water over his head "in the name of the Father and of the Son and of the Holy Spirit." The child's white garment symbolizes that he has "put on Christ" (Gal. 3:27 ESV), and a candle, lit from the Easter candle, signifies the illumination of the new creation. Through this rite of initiation, those who are baptized are forgiven of sin and born again in the Holy Spirit. This gift, which is unmerited, is called "initial justification."[31]

With the process of justification underway through the sacramental system, one begins to merit for himself the graces needed to attain eternal life. Through the Eucharist (the consecrated wafer of the Lord's Supper), additional grace is infused into one's soul by the Holy Spirit which heals and sanctifies it. This growth in justification is fed by the "eucharistic sacrifice of Christ," that is, the ongoing sacrifice of the Mass in which Christ offers himself to the Father at the heavenly altar. This sacrifice is understood as perpetuated through time from Jesus' death at Calvary to the present.[32] Thus, as Christ offered himself directly to the Father from the cross, he is thought to also do so in the Mass through the hands of the priest, such that "[t]he sacrifice of Christ and the sacrifice of the Eucharist are *one single sacrifice*."[33] By receiving the Eucharist, one preserves, increases, and renews the life of grace that is received at baptism.

When a Catholic commits a so-called mortal sin — a serious transgression which causes him to fall away from God — he must observe the rite of reconciliation (also called the sacrament of penance or confession). This is done by expressing repentance, contrition (genuine sorrow over one's sin), and confession to a priest. Upon hearing the confession, the priest forgives (which is called "absolution") in the name of Jesus and determines the manner of "satisfaction" (reparation for sin through such activities as prayer, an offering, works of mercy, service, or self-denial). Through this process, one who has fallen away from salvation may be re-justified (or reborn again) and thus restored to friendship with God.

If an individual successfully reaches the end of life in a state of grace (that is, he is not guilty of a mortal sin), he will ultimately be saved. Chances are, however, that he will have to first spend a period of time in "purgatory," an experience of suffering that involves punishment.[34] Purgatory also has a sanctifying effect, conforming one to the holiness of God. When men and women have passed through purgatory, they are finally prepared to enter the presence of God in heaven.[35]

There are numerous ways to compare the Roman Catholic and evangelical Protestant approaches to salvation. Once again, our common commitments are significant. We agree, for instance, that salvation is Trinitarian: The Father declares sinful man to be righteous, upon the merits and saving grace of Christ, by the regenerating work of the Holy Spirit.[36] We believe that salvation is rooted in history, with implications that are spiritual and moral. We affirm that justification has been merited for us by Jesus Christ, whose blood atones for our sins. And we recognize the aim of salvation to be the realization of holiness in service of the glory of God.[37]

For all of our similarities, however, we also have important differences. Our fundamental disagreement concerns the reason why God ultimately accepts us. For the Catholic, this acceptance is the culmination of a religious journey, a faithful life nurtured by the sacraments in which one grows in grace. In the course of growing, one merits divine favor and, by doing so, eventually receives the divine declaration of acceptance.[38] While initial grace of salvation cannot be merited, according to Catholic teaching, faithful men and women merit for themselves and for others all the graces needed to obtain eternal life.[39]

Evangelical Protestants, on the other hand, recognize fallen humanity as incapable of securing even the smallest amount of divine merit by performing good works. We consider our most noble attempts as unworthy of the glory of God. Instead, divine acceptance is based on the perfection of Christ's righteousness which is accounted to the sinner (Rom. 4). Remember Luther's dung metaphor. Because we are clothed in Christ's perfection, God regards us as fully righteous. Unlike the Catholic system, in which the decisive verdict of God's acceptance comes at the end of life following the accumulation of sacramental grace, evangelical Protestants typically emphasize the decisive moment when an individual believes in the gospel by faith alone. From a Reformed Protestant point of view, this results in a permanent conversion in which one becomes a child of God.[40] Of course, children are occasionally disciplined, but they are not disowned by loving parents. For this reason, one's relationship to God is secure.

Once converted, children of God participate in a journey toward holiness called sanctification. Regarding the necessity of this process, Paul the apostle says:

> But now he has reconciled you by Christ's physical body through death to present you holy in his sight, without blemish and free from accusation — *if you continue in your faith*, established and firm, and do not move from the hope held out in the gospel (Col. 1:22 – 23, emphasis added).

Notice Paul's qualification: "if you continue in your faith." Such perseverance is necessary to authenticate the reality of one's faith, without which one demonstrates that he or she was never genuinely converted in the first place. For evangelical Protestants who don't have a Reformed outlook on salvation, such texts indicate that it is possible to lose salvation. In either instance, the Protestant vision insists that while justification is secured by faith alone, it is a faith that never remains alone since the Holy Spirit lives within God's children.

It is not enough to simply distinguish the Catholic and Protestant positions. We must also step back to reflect on values and concerns which drive them. For example, why do Catholics stress the need for good works in justification? How can Protestants of different denominations claim to possess a unified faith? And why does it sound like presumption, from a Catholic perspective, to express assurance of one's salvation? Such questions yield insight into the other tradition, which inevitably help us to be more effective communicators of the gospel. Our next chapter will examine such questions.

We have covered a lot of ground in this chapter, and I commend you for persevering to the end! Hopefully, it has provided a sharper perspective on where the lines of continuity and difference fall between Roman Catholic and evangelical Protestant belief. With such lessons in mind, we now proceed to consider some practical implications of these differences for religious discussion among our Catholic friends and loved ones.

CHAPTER FIVE

EMBODYING AND PROCLAIMING THE GOSPEL

I n this chapter we will consider the practical dimensions of gospel witness among Catholics. Because there is no such thing as a view from nowhere, it is important that we evaluate how the beliefs of Catholics (covered in our previous chapter) either support or undermine evangelism. In doing so, I hope to maximize common ground as a fruitful starting point to conversation, while at the same time avoiding the land mines that inevitably detonate when we fail to consider our differences. Such consideration will focus on the two fundamental issues covered in our previous chapter (authority and salvation), since they have such profound and far-reaching implications for Christian life.

Let's start by thinking about salvation. Consider a classic land mine on which we often step: our message that justification is by "faith alone." From an evangelical Protestant perspective, the fact that our ultimate acceptance comes by faith apart from human works is about as central as it gets to the good news of the gospel. Why then does it *not* sound so good to Catholic ears? This is where some familiarity with the doctrinal underpinning of the issue is valuable. Given the Catholic assumptions concerning justification—that it is a *process* in which one becomes increasingly righteous—the assertion that God accepts us by faith alone often sounds like "cheap grace" (to borrow a phrase from Dietrich Bonhoeffer). It sounds like we're saying, "Don't worry about pursuing a life of holiness. Just say this sinner's prayer, walk this aisle, and then you'll be safe for all of eternity." Thus, for Catholics, our doctrine of salvation resembles a form of fire insurance that requires a minimal investment in exchange for an eternal payoff.

So what is happening here? On one side, evangelical Protestants are sharing one of the most glorious and beautiful truths that they possess—the message that God, like the father of the prodigal son in Luke 15, wraps his loving arms around us despite the filthiness of our sin; meanwhile, to Catholics it sounds like a bunch of rubbish that diminishes divine holiness and reduces salvation to a momentary experience. I shudder to think of how many gospel conversations have been blown to smithereens by this land mine.

How then can we improve communication on this issue? It is up to evangelical Protestants to "contextualize" the message of faith alone so that Catholics can understand precisely what we are *not* saying. For example, when I discuss salvation with a Catholic friend, I seek to emphasize that while it is impossible to merit even the smallest measure of divine favor, we are nonetheless called to manifest holiness as God's new creation in Christ (2 Cor. 5:17), for such devotion to Christ is basic to our Christian identity. Unfortunately, in our zeal to emphasize the grace of justification, we can easily ignore the work of the Spirit in sanctification. The tragic result is a truncated portrait of salvation. Is it any wonder that Catholics often find our message lopsided?

SPEAKING THE SAME LANGUAGE

What should we do about it? We must tell the whole story, that is, we must remain forthright concerning faith alone, and equally forthright about the need to pursue holiness. Paul the apostle makes this point beautifully in Ephesians 2:8–10:

> For it is by grace you have been saved, through faith—and this is not from yourselves, it is the gift of God—not by works, so that no one can boast. For we are God's handiwork, created in Christ Jesus to do good works, which God prepared in advance for us to do.

Simply put, the God who accepts us by grace through faith also shapes us into the image of Christ. You can't have one without the other. A sensitive and more promising approach to gospel communication among Catholics will adequately account for both sides of the equation.

A close second to the subject of faith alone is the challenge of discussing the issue of "eternal security," the belief that when God justifies an individual, he causes that person to faithfully persevere to the end.[1] For Catholics, such assurance sounds presumptuous. Why is this so? It is a function of the fact that Catholic doctrine looks forward to the end of life to discover whether one is finally accepted as a child of God. With such a perspective, it is difficult to conceive of salvation as eternally secure.

Can we agree that there is some validity to these Catholic concerns? Too often evangelical Protestants unwittingly treat the idea of eternal security flippantly. We have all met the "born again" person who only comes to church on Easter but nonetheless believes he is assured of his salvation because he once raised his hand as a child to accept Christ as his personal Savior. This is presumption. Such false security has no place in Christian faith. Perhaps you and the mature people of your congregation avoid this error, but I am afraid that a good deal of Evangelicalism-at-large is culpable. It is therefore appropriate for us to take ownership of the caricature and seek to correct it. I like how theologian Tony Lane captures the desired balance when he states that our doctrine of salvation must retain the tension between Luke 18:9–14 and Luke 14:25–33:

> In the parable of the Pharisee and the tax collector it is not the one who can point to his works who is justified but the one who prays, 'God, have mercy on me, a sinner.' Yet against this must be set the uncompromising

teaching that 'any of you who does not give up everything he has cannot be my disciple.' There is a sharp
tension between these two passages [that must be
upheld].[2]

How about the issue of authority? It has been said,
rightly I think, that Catholic reflection on God leads one
to concentrate upon the sacramental life of the church,
whereas the evangelical Protestant typically stresses the
doctrine of salvation. This tendency may be observed,
for example, by the way we arrange furniture in our
churches. For instance, when you enter an evangelical
Protestant church building, what do you see front and
center? It is generally the pulpit on which the preacher
sets his Bible to preach the text. And what do you observe
front and center when you enter a Catholic parish? You
see the altar where the priest consecrates the host in the
celebration of Eucharist. Thus, the Protestant doctrine of
Scripture alone (centering on the Bible) and the Catholic
teaching on continuous incarnation (focusing on communion) finds tangible expression.

Implications of our respective views on authority
are numerous. For starters, it is one of the reasons why
Catholics look at the proliferation of Protestant denominations with utter incredulity. If the fullness of Christian
faith is found in communion with the one holy catholic
and apostolic Church, and Protestants willfully separate from that communion, it is natural for Catholics
to view Protestant Christianity as inferior. Furthermore,
since Catholics generally think of apostolic faith as having an institutional shape, there is hardly any other way

of viewing the lack of unity between various Protestant denominations than to question their validity. Communion is crucial, and Protestants are perceived as being rather bankrupt in this area.

I say "perceived" because the picture looks different from an evangelical Protestant point of view. For the Evangelical, it is not the institutional affiliation that matters most (i.e., one's denomination), important as it is. Of greater importance is a commitment to the central message of the gospel. For example, on the same street you may have Presbyterian, Anglican, Baptist, Pentecostal, and Methodist churches, but to the extent that they maintain a gospel-centered approach to ministry, there is, from an Evangelical's point of view, a genuine bond of unity between them. In this instance, adherence to Scripture (particularly its message of salvation) is the chief characteristic that defines solidarity. Such a value is traceable to the Protestant commitment to biblical authority.

Here is another way to think about it. I once overheard a conversation between a Catholic and a Protestant on how the Bible forms Christian faith and practice. The Protestant used the metaphor of a sailboat to argue for the doctrine of Scripture alone. Traditions that can't be explicitly supported by Scripture, he argued, are like barnacles on the hull of the boat. Just as the accumulation of barnacles inevitably damage the boat and decrease its forward progress, unbiblical traditions injure the faith and retard the advance of the gospel. After a moment of thought, the Catholic responded by explaining that what the Protestant called "barnacles" was in fact *the ship*. To remove such traditions from the life of the church would destroy the beautiful texture of the Christian faith, he argued. The conversation helped me to see that one man's barnacle is another man's boat, depending on our view of authority.

The practical outworking of our ecclesiology (our understanding of the Church, including its use of authority) has implications for discussion among Catholic friends. Just as we Evangelicals are susceptible to emphasizing faith alone to the exclusion of obedience in salvation, we are likewise at risk of stressing personal (individualized) faith at the expense of our corporate identity. Such a narrow approach, however, is to ignore that we also enjoy participation in a faith community. As the body of Christ we are "members" belonging to one another (Rom. 12:3–8), or, to use another biblical metaphor, we are "living stones" with which God constructs a spiritual house (1 Peter 2:5). When talking with Catholics, it is important to capture this communal dimension of our identity, even as we celebrate the glorious benefits that we enjoy as individuals.

PRINCIPLES FOR GOSPEL WITNESS
When proclaiming and embodying gospel truth among Catholic friends, it is helpful to follow some guiding principles that promise to strengthen our witness:

1. PUT LOVE FIRST
It is easy to remember the "first and greatest commandment": "Love the Lord your God with all your heart and

with all your soul and with all your mind." But it can be harder—especially in the heat of sharing our most deeply held convictions—to remember the second, even though Jesus says it is like the first: "Love your neighbor as yourself."[3] As mentioned earlier, no matter how strong our desire to defend biblical truth, we must remember that loving our neighbor, who is made in God's image, is of inestimable importance.

2. PUT PEOPLE BEFORE PROOFS

Sheer evidence rarely convinces people; truth embedded in relationships does. We know this based on our own experiences. While it is certainly important to understand the reasons for our faith and to develop the ability to express biblical truth cogently, we must remember that our conversations with Catholics are more than apologetic interactions; they are relationships in which we have the privilege of communicating the good news of Jesus. On some occasions this will call for a systematic presentation of evidence and may involve debate. Terrific. But we do so with the understanding that our interaction is aimed at serving our Catholic friend, not "defeating" him or her.

3. ABSTAIN FROM THE EUCHARIST

Receiving the Eucharist may be natural for you, especially if you are a former Catholic and think that abstaining from the host may now cause confusion among your Catholic friends and family. However, we must remember that for Catholics the sacrament of communion is considered to be more than a memorial or spiritual encounter with Christ; it is the actual body of Christ. By partaking of the elements, you are assuming communion with the Catholic Church, affirming that the bread and wine are actually the body and blood of Jesus Christ. It is best, therefore, out of respect for the tenets of the Catholic Church and for your own Protestant convictions, to abstain from receiving the sacrament.

4. WATCH YOUR WORDS

In many languages there are identical words but with entirely different meanings from one culture to the next. This is often true of words and phrases used by Catholics and Protestants. Rather than assuming that we share a common meaning by our words, we ought to understand their differences. Here are a few examples.

Some evangelical terminology is entirely foreign to Catholic ears. Usually, Catholics (notwithstanding the evangelical Catholic) don't talk about being "saved" or "born again." If a traditional or cultural Catholic speaks this way, he will likely have infant baptism in mind. Likewise, it's unlikely you'll hear the words "witness," "devotions" (or "devotionals"), "fellowship," "believer," "small group," "evangelism," or "quiet time" used by Catholics. In short, it's wise to avoid tribal language that's unique to one's evangelical circle but incomprehensible to outsiders.

While much of this nomenclature can simply confuse or create misunderstanding between Catholics and Protestants, some terminology can actually sound offensive. For instance, Evangelicals may draw a contrast between one who is "Christian" versus "Catholic." This reference may be nothing more than shorthand for a distinction that is otherwise too complicated to explain in the moment. However, to Catholic ears, it often sounds like we are suggesting that Catholics are categorically un-Christian. Therefore, in my humble opinion, such a dichotomy is best avoided, even if, on occasion, we hear it from Catholics themselves.

5. Remember Your Family Roots

If you were raised Catholic, communicating your religious convictions to family members who have known you since birth is an especially delicate matter. The uncle who taught you how to catch a pop-fly or the aunt who used to wipe your nose may not take kindly to you educating them about God. Rather than speaking to these loved ones in what *may be perceived* as a condescending manner, you want to work extra hard to communicate the gospel with deference and respect.

6. Keep Your Cool

When people discuss matters of ultimate importance for their lives, emotions naturally run high. This is especially true when faith is inextricably linked to one's culture and family, as is true for many Catholics. Bursts of passion will inevitably occur, but we must never allow them to approach impatience or anger. This doesn't mean holding back from sharing the depth of our convictions, but it does mean remembering, even when the temperature rises, that our friends and loved ones treasure their convictions just as much as we treasure ours. We must therefore exercise great humility and meekness.

7. EXTEND GENUINE CONCERN FOR YOUR CATHOLIC FRIEND

The writer C. S. Lewis provides a good example of the attitude of sincere love with which we ought to approach our Catholic friends and loved ones. In a letter to a friend who had recently converted to Catholicism, he expressed his feelings about her faith with honesty and respect, balancing his own convictions with obedience to the call to love his neighbor as himself:

> It is a little difficult to explain how I feel that though you have taken a way which is not for me, I nevertheless can congratulate you—I suppose because of your faith and joy which are so obviously increased. Naturally, I do not draw from that the same conclusions as you—but there is no need for us to start a controversial correspondence! I believe that we are very dear to one another but not because I am at all on the Rome-ward frontier of my own communion. I believe that in the present divided state of Christendom, those who are at the heart of each division are closer to one another than those who are at the fringes.[4]

8. EXPRESS GENUINE REVERENCE FOR GOD

One thing that perplexes Catholics about Evangelicals is our tendency to appear, as they see it, "overly chummy" with God. Our emphasis on the intimate nature of God's love and personal relationship with Christ are important values that serve to invigorate faith; however, it is important to remember, especially in communication with our Catholic friends, that this intimate Lord is also our terrifying God, a "consuming fire."[5] The Catholic perspective is generally more along these lines, and is well articulated by the writer Annie Dillard:

> On the whole, I do not find Christians, outside the catacombs, sufficiently sensible of the conditions [of God's presence]. Does anyone have the foggiest idea what sort of power we so blithely invoke? Or, as I suspect, does no one believe a word of it? The churches are children playing on the floor with their chemistry sets, mixing up a batch of TNT to kill a Sunday morning. It is madness to wear ladies' straw hats and velvet hats to church; we should all be wearing crash helmets. Ushers should issue life preservers and signal flares; they should lash us to our pews. For the sleeping god may wake some day and take offense; or the waking god may draw us out to where we can never return.[6]

9. VALUE BIBLICAL UNITY

The Catholic Church is a faith community united by common structures of liturgy and parish life under a singular magisterial authority. Evangelicals, on the other hand, tend to epitomize the values of independence and individualism. Where Evangelicals may see the benefits of a loose network of leaders who sharpen one another through collaboration and ongoing discussion of biblical interpretation, Catholics often see a fragmented system characterized by doctrinal disagreement. It is therefore important that among fellow Christians we express our commitment to preserving the unity of the Spirit in the bond of peace (Eph. 4:3).

10. EXHIBIT A GENUINE LOVE FOR JESUS

It was on an airplane from Rome to London that I sat beside Father John. A member of the Curia (the adminis-tration of the Holy See), John is an American priest who works in the Vatican and teaches theology. Before the plane reached the runway for takeoff, we found ourselves engrossed in conversation on a wide range of issues, everything from Vatican II to our favorite rock music. Since John and I are the same age, we easily connected. The entire flight was full of warm-hearted discussion.

Thanks to the wonder of email, John and I have enjoyed keeping in touch over the years. I have learned a lot from reading some of his publications, and, on account of his personal advice, I matriculated into a Ph.D. program, a course of study that I may not have considered without his encouragement. These are a couple of ways that John has been a grace in my life. But let me tell the most profound way of all. Because John is one of those remarkably humble guys, a man who appears to live in conscious surrender to Christ, I have found myself inspired by his example of piety. In short, he is the kind of person whose behavior makes you want to be more like Jesus.

So here is the lesson. Of all the things we can say and do among Catholic friends, the most important and enduring is to maintain authentic devotion to Christ. There is something unmistakable about a man or a woman who walks with the living God. The fragrance of the Spirit is obvious in such a one, and among onlookers it is infectious. It doesn't matter how well I preach biblical truth, for instance, if I don't convey the beauty of Christ's character. On the other hand, with holy aspirations consecrated in service to the living God, we will find ourselves manifesting the most compelling quality: the aroma of Christ.

CONCLUSION

At the top of St. Mary's Church in Krakow, Poland, where I stood a few years ago after attending a conference, a lone herald sounded the trumpet. These days it simply marks the passing of another hour, but in previous centuries, the trumpet was played by the city guard to warn people of fires and other dangers, such as the arrival of hostile armies. It was a steel-tipped arrow from one such army that pierced the throat of the herald in 1257, but not before he had sounded the alarm: the city gates were closed and many lives were saved. You can still hear the tune played every hour, on the hour, but it is deliberately and abruptly cut short to commemorate the death of Krakow's brave trumpeter.

As I gazed up at St. Mary's balcony, considering how important it was for the herald to sound the alarm, I couldn't help but think about our calling to herald the message of Christ, a calling that reaches back to the Church's inception. This is how the earliest followers of Christ, men and women very much like us, lived their lives. They constituted a small minority in a hostile pagan culture and were reviled because of their allegiance to Christ. Arrested and jailed, hauled before pagan magistrates, hated, ridiculed, and even martyred, they were held in contempt by the world for persevering in gospel proclamation. Two thousand years later, the Church is pursuing the same calling. Despite the fact that we are often pilloried in the media, marginalized in the academy, and dismissed by the cultural elite, we remain busy preaching the message of Christ.

God help us to share this good news with the same degree of urgency and wisdom, even as Paul describes in 1 Corinthians: "For Jews demand signs and Greeks seek wisdom, but we preach Christ crucified, a stumbling block to Jews and folly to Gentiles, but to those who are called, both Jews and Greeks, Christ the power of God and the wisdom of God" (1 Corinthians 1:22–24 ESV).

CHAPTER SIX

THE TOP TEN QUESTIONS ABOUT CATHOLICISM

Over my years of ministry among former Catholics, the same or similar questions have emerged repeatedly from individuals who live at the Catholic-Protestant intersection. I often read them in emails, hear them in counseling sessions, and watch them fill the "comments" section of blog posts. Of them all, the following ten appear to represent the biggest concerns. Some of these questions are of a more relational nature; others are more doctrinal.

Question 1: How can Protestant churches be more welcoming of Catholics and former Catholics on Sunday morning?

As a pastor of outreach for nearly a decade, this question occupied the foreground of my thinking for a long time.

Here are several practical ways to welcome Catholics as Protestant church members.

- *Avoid using cheesy clichés from the evangelical subculture.* We Evangelicals are marketing champions. We can baptize American pop culture into the Christian realm faster than you can say Testamints®. When it is done responsibly, we call it "contextualization." Yet all too often it happens at the expense of God's holiness and feels like we have reduced the Lord of Glory to a product. Whether we are employing a hackneyed phrase of dubious theological substance or a general ethos that speaks of divine realities with flippancy, we must remember that God is the Almighty One who abides in unapproachable light and therefore deserves the utmost reverence.

- *Offer page numbers of your sermon texts, if you have pew Bibles.* Many Catholics have not had the opportunity to study the Bible. When first stepping into a Protestant church, some of them will hardly know the difference between the Old and New Testaments, much less where to find a certain chapter and verse. Offering page numbers of your sermon texts is a simple courtesy that enables former Catholics to follow along. I can remember my first visit to a Protestant church on my native Long Island, where the preacher had us turn to Romans before looking at Hebrews. In my biblically illiterate mind, I can remember thinking, *Romans is written especially for me, because I am Italian; Hebrews, on the other hand, must be for my Jewish friends.* I am certain that most Catholics are more knowledgeable than I was. But, then again, in some instances maybe not much more.

- *Speak of the Catholic Church with courtesy, especially at points of disagreement.* Anti-Catholicism has a deep, abiding history in the United States. Even among good-natured Protestants, it is common to hear sharp invectives launched against the Catholic Church. Such an approach is wrong for several reasons: First, theologically, it fails to convey the redemptive character of our Lord Jesus Christ, the One who was full of grace and truth (John 1:14). Second, it undermines relationships with our Catholic friends. Third, it ignores the fact that over the course of time the Catholic Church has accomplished great good in the world. Whether translating Scripture, serving the poor, or protecting the unborn, there is much of the Catholic legacy for which evangelical Protestants can give thanks.

- *Explain biblical concepts and terminology in a way that is clear and accessible.* It is easy for us Evangelicals, particularly pastors, to speak "the language of Zion," forgetting that many folks in today's post-Christian world, Catholics *and* Protestants, have not a clue what we are saying. It is fine to speak of "Adam Christology" or "the eschatological substructure of the *parousia*"; however, be sure to define such terms and offer a reasonable

explanation of their meanings. Everyone benefits
from clear communication.

- *Convey genuine remorse over the divided state of the
  Church.* In his book *The Riddle of Roman Catholicism,* Jaroslav Pelikan famously described the
  Reformation as a "tragic necessity," recognizing
  that the sixteenth-century Church needed reform.
  Yet the subsequent division struck a massive blow
  to the Church's integrity, particularly in the eyes of
  the world. This tragedy is something that pastors
  should recognize, faithfully looking forward to the
  day when Jesus will return to unify his body.

- *Be serious about cultural engagement and uphold an
  ethic of life.* As we have seen, the idea of "incarnation," in terms of tangibly manifesting God's
  mercy, is a core value of Catholic theology and
  tends to be of importance at the local parish level.
  Therefore, most Catholics are taught to put a high
  premium on practical forms of service; application
  of moral imperatives; and advocacy for the vulnerable in society such as the unborn and elderly.
  To the extent that Catholics are indeed faithful
  to their tradition, they will pursue these ends.
  Protestant churches, motivated by the incarnation
  impulse of the New Testament, must do the same.

- *Demonstrate that you believe what you believe.*
  Hypocrisy is a problem in every religious context.
  It is unavoidable when following Jesus, the perfect God/man; we all fall short of his glory. Yet
  some forms of hypocrisy are egregious: Protestants

condemn moral failure in the priesthood and Catholics point to the shameful behavior of some of our "televangelists." For every critical finger we point, several are pointing back at us. Therefore, whenever possible, we must take responsibility for our shortcomings and for that of our churches, avoiding hypocrisy on the personal and corporate levels.

• *Express reverence and authenticity when you pray.* Prayer is serious business. We all know this, and yet sometimes we Evangelicals appear to saunter into God's presence, express a few platitudes of praise, throw down some personal requests, and conclude in Christ's name. Yes, Jesus called his disciples "friends" three times in John 15, emphasizing the personal nature of their faith. At the same time, John the apostle, when confronted by the risen and glorified Christ, fell down as a dead man (Rev. 1:17). Our prayers should reflect both of these realities, joy and a fearful sobriety.

Question 2: What do you think about Catholics and Protestants dating with a view to marriage?

"For never was a story of more woe, than this of Juliet and her Romeo."[1] The span of William Shakespeare's famous protagonists' affection across the contentious divide of the warring Montague and Capulet families has inspired hearts for centuries. And after the star-crossed lovers met their fate, and their reconciled families cracked open a bottle of Chianti, we proceeded to relish the warmth and pain of other dramas: from Jets and Sharks dancing on the West Side to lovers in the frigid water surrounding the sinking *Titanic*. The storyline is familiar: Love found. Love lost. Love regained, only to be lost again.

One need not serve long in pastoral ministry before he or she encounters romantic tragedies in the congregation. These, however, are not to be relished. With deep sorrow, I have observed two couples whom I married later divorce. It is heartbreaking. Such experiences cause us to consider the factors that either serve or undermine a marriage. This consideration eventually leads to Paul's words in 2 Corinthians 6:14, his memorable statement about "not be[ing] unequally yoked with unbelievers" (ESV). This truth is part of Relationship Building 101, for "what partnership has light with darkness?" Then someone responds: "Yes, but what if one person in the couple is an Evangelical and the other one is a Catholic, disagreeing on some things to be sure, but otherwise standing together on a common Nicene faith?" Good question.

Perhaps it is because I have written on the topic of things Catholic and Protestant that I am frequently asked for advice on this subject. Such questions reach me through email or come walking into my office, often amid tears. They are not questions to be taken lightly; indeed, the responses can influence the trajectory of two lives and two faiths.

I remember one particular wedding. An amber glow upon the bride's and groom's faces, illumined by the candles on the altar table behind me, showcased the gravity of the moment. Having grown up together at College Church in Wheaton, they were now getting married. Their sweaty palms, nervous smiles, and mutual pledges of love and fidelity captivated the attention of onlookers. "From this day forth, as long as we both shall live," they resolutely confessed. With those words our minds were drawn to the cross of Christ, the covenant that it established, and the cosmic calling of this couple to bear witness to God's kingdom. "This mystery [of marriage] is profound, and I'm saying that it refers to Christ and his church," Paul said (Eph. 5:32 ESV).

Such was the backdrop for my counseling session with a different young woman the following day. Ann's situation turned out to be simpler than most. Precisely because of the biblical admonition expressed in 2 Corinthians 6, she had already broken up with her boyfriend on account of their varied faith commitments. He was Catholic, she was Protestant. "We're not equally yoked," she exclaimed. "What else could I have done?" Apparently, the man Ann was dating didn't understand why their relationship was terminal. Ann wanted advice from me on how to give an answer for the nuptial hope within her.

In counseling Ann, I had two objectives: I wanted the gospel to illumine her decision to end the relationship, and I also wanted to enrich her perspective on what it will look like to one day accept a man's proposal for marriage. Starting with the first, I affirmed that it is possible for Catholics to be born-again Christians who love Jesus and genuinely seek to serve him. In the words of Philip Ryken:

> Sometimes we forget that Luther, Calvin, and the rest of the Reformers were born and bred within the Roman church. When Catholics were catholic, they were Catholic too, and it was within the Roman church that they came to saving faith in Jesus Christ. To be sure, the pope would not tolerate their plain teaching of the gospel, so eventually they were thrown out of the church. But God can and does carry out his saving work to this day, even where his gospel is not preached in all its clarity.[2]

As Ryken explains, there may be Catholics who have experienced salvation while resisting the evangelical doctrines of grace. Valid as this faith may be, however, it does not mean that such a man is suited for a young woman who is seeking to live her life according to the Bible. To the extent that this Catholic recognizes the authority and revelation of Christ to be in and from the institution of the Catholic Church, the yoke is unequal. And this leads me to my second point.

The bar must be higher than simply finding a "Christian man." I told Ann, "You want a guy who is devoted to the Word, who is captivated by the triune God; someone whose life is defined by redemptive grace from top to bottom, who embodies it, proclaims it, and understands his marital calling in terms of shepherding you by this grace. And, if the Lord should one day bless you with children, realize that this man will be one of the two people who most influence your family's spiritual life.

You're not looking for perfection, but he must demonstrate a credible trajectory toward gospel priorities."

Let's be honest: a large number of evangelical men in our churches don't fit this bill. I am not for a moment suggesting that the community of godly marriage candidates is found across the Protestant border. What I am saying is that women and men who are considering marriage must be sober-minded in their assessment of the spiritual maturity of their prospective spouses, a maturity that relates directly to the person's commitment to God's Word.

At a Wheaton College dialogue that I moderated, featuring Timothy George, Dean of Beeson Divinity School, and Frank Beckwith, a high-profile convert from Evangelicalism to Catholicism, Frank was asked how to think about a Catholic and Protestant relationship en route to marriage. Frank's answer (from a Catholic perspective) was extremely helpful. He pointed out the manifold challenges awaiting such couples, not least of which is the requisite pledge of the non-Catholic spouse to raise his or her children in the Catholic Church. Frank suggested that couples don't always think seriously about the complexities and inevitable confusion that these mixed marriages create— everything from a divergent understanding of sacramental theology to a different approach to worship. "We have to take our theology seriously," Beckwith said, "and that means that doing the right thing is sometimes unpleasant."

Although Catholics and Protestants stand together in a common Nicene faith, it is not with a unified voice. Our interpretation of the "one holy catholic and apostolic

Church," as we have considered, differs at critical points, resulting in basic disagreements of faith and practice. Where we enjoy unity, let's not be afraid to recognize it. But where such unity is absent, we must have the courage to acknowledge that as well. Marriage, precisely because of its covenantal nature, must be a place in which these differences are addressed with honesty and fidelity.

Question 3: How can evangelical Protestants better understand the Catholic Mass?

Theologians have the prerogative to make distinctions. It is how seminaries train us; it is the currency with which we trade. Among theologians, few excel in formulating and articulating the subtleties of doctrine like our Catholic friends, and the mystery of the Mass is a place where this is especially observed. As a "mystery," the Catholic Mass is by definition beyond human comprehension. Yet when Protestants explain what happens in the Mass, we often get it wrong, propagating misunderstandings that directly contradict the explicit teaching of the Catholic Church. Addressing the issue intelligently and persuasively requires us to understand the following concepts. If effectiveness in ministry is related to upholding truth and avoiding straw men, these lessons should be noted.

MISUNDERSTANDING ONE: CATHOLICS TEACH THAT CHRIST IS "PHYSICALLY PRESENT" IN THE MASS

When describing Jesus Christ in the Eucharist, Catholics will say that the Lord is "really," "truly," "wholly," "continuously," or "substantially" present, but *not* "physically." To say that Jesus is "physically" present is to suggest that he is present "locally" (as he is now in heaven at the right hand of the Father). The eucharistic presence of Christ, although understood as no less real, is a sacramental presence in the (transubstantiated) host. From the *Catechism of the Catholic Church*:

> **1413** By the consecration the transubstantiation of the bread and wine into the Body and Blood of Christ is brought about. Under the consecrated species of bread and wine Christ himself, living and glorious, is present in a true, real, and substantial manner: his Body and his Blood, with his soul and his divinity (cf. Council of Trent: DS 1640; 1651).[3]

MISUNDERSTANDING TWO: CATHOLICS TEACH THAT CHRIST IS RE-SACRIFICED AT THE MASS

This is perhaps the most common misconception. If I had a dime for every pastor friend I've heard say that the Mass is a repetition of the cross, I might have enough money for a cappuccino at Starbucks. It is permissible to say that the Mass is a repetition of the Last Supper, but not of Jesus' cross. Catholic doctrine teaches that the Mass "renews" or "re-presents" the cross; but it doesn't "repeat" it. Catholic tradition asserts that in a mystical and sacramental sense, the Mass *is* the cross, the once-and-for-all offering of God's Son continued through time. For those of you who have studied grammar, it's like an ingressive aorist: the description of an action that has been completed and is also ongoing. Or it is, if you will, like a golf putt. Please pardon the comparison of the supremely glorious cross with the banality of golf, but when I swing my putter at the ball, the initial contact is the "putt." At the same time, the action of the ball rolling toward the pin (and in my case, *past* the pin) is also the "putt." The putt has happened *and* is happening. So the sacrifice of Jesus is completed (hence, informed Catholics know how to explain Jesus' words "it is finished") and it is also ongoing. Again, from the Catechism:

> **1407** The Eucharist is the heart and the summit of the Church's life, for in it Christ associates his Church and all her members with his sacrifice of praise and thanksgiving offered once for all on the cross to his Father; by this sacrifice he pours out the graces of salvation on his Body which is the Church.

MISUNDERSTANDING THREE: CATHOLICS TEACH THAT CHRIST DIES AT THE MASS

This misunderstanding is closely related to the second one. If one regards the Mass as a re-sacrifice, then, logically, he will view that sacrifice as constituting another death. However, according to the Catholic Church, Christ doesn't "die" in the Mass; he is "immolated." For some Protestants that will be a new term. "Immolation" comes from the Latin *immolare*, "to sacrifice." Simply put, in the Mass, when the priest elevates the wafer and recites the words of consecration, Jesus is presented as the Victim who died for our sins.

> **1366** The Eucharist is thus a sacrifice because it *represents* (makes present) the sacrifice of the cross, because it is its *memorial* and because it *applies* its fruit:

[Christ], our Lord and God, was once and for all to offer himself to God the Father by his death on the altar of the cross, to accomplish there an everlasting redemption. But because his priesthood was not to end with his death, at the Last Supper "on the night when he was betrayed," [he wanted] to leave to his beloved spouse the Church a visible sacrifice (as the nature of man demands) by which the bloody sacrifice which he was to accomplish once for all on the cross would be re-presented, its memory perpetuated until the end of the world, and its salutary power be applied to the forgiveness of the sins we daily commit.

The implications of the above are numerous. First, it explains why Catholics display the crucifix—the figure of Jesus upon the cross. It also highlights how different are the Catholic and Protestant understandings of "propitiation" (the act of appeasing God's wrath, which results in evading judgment and receiving divine favor). I have heard theologians argue that this issue of the eucharistic sacrifice of Christ is a more substantial difference between Catholics and Protestants than our disagreement over the relationship between faith and works.

I want to underscore the need for Protestants to use the proper terms. You know that feeling when you hear a person reduce the doctrine of faith alone to nothing more than mere cheap grace (i.e., walk an aisle, say a prayer, live like an antinomian slug)? It is inaccurate and unfair, and your respect for such a person's argument is naturally diminished. This is essentially what happens among our Catholic brothers and sisters when we misrepresent the Mass. Fruitful gospel conversations require us to get the details straight.

Question 4: In light of the Decrees of Trent (1545–1563), which oppose the Protestant doctrine of justification by faith alone, wouldn't we have to say that official Catholic doctrine on the matter of salvation rises to the level of error so serious that it amounts to "another gospel" — thus warranting an apostolic anathema (statement of condemnation)?

The most helpful book I have read on this topic is *Justification by Faith in Catholic-Protestant Dialogue: An Evangelical Assessment* by Tony Lane, professor of historical theology at London School of Theology. Here are some of Lane's responses that have bearing on the above question. The word "Tridentine" in this context simply describes ideas that come to us from the Council of Trent.

Is the positive exposition of the Tridentine decree compatible with a Protestant understanding?

"No. When the difference in terminology is taken into account and when allowance is made for complementary formulations, the gap turns out to be considerably narrower than is often popularly supposed, but a gap there remains."[4]

Do the Tridentine canons condemn the Protestant doctrine or only parodies of it?

"Many of the canons do not directly touch a balanced Protestant understanding, but a number clearly do."[5]

According to Lane, disagreement between the Catholic

and Protestant understanding of justification persists, although it may not be as profound as we sometimes think. Still, given the binding nature of Trent's decrees, the Reformed doctrine of "faith alone" continues to be officially anathematized, or condemned, by the Catholic Church. To the extent that Catholics press this Tridentine framework (i.e., defining their position over and against justification by faith alone), they may find themselves skating on the same thin ice as the Judaizers of Galatia and in danger of falling into the frigid water of Paul's critique.

It is also valuable to remember another of Professor Lane's points, though. Speaking about the particular target(s) of Trent's teaching, he writes, "The canons [of Trent] were deliberately not addressed against specific people and the statements condemned were derived from second- or third-hand compilations of the statements of the Reformers, taken especially from the earlier years of the Reformation and not seen in their original context."[6] Thus, unlike Alexander V's papal bull against Wycliffism in 1409 or Leo X's *Exsurge Domine* against Luther in 1520, Trent's canons were aiming into a mist of hearsay (not to be confused with the word "heresy"). Moving forward in history, even to the present, Catholic theologians have said, in effect, that because the bishops of Trent misunderstood aspects of Reformation teaching, the object of their canons were different from what truly was or is Protestant theology. Accordingly, the preamble of the Joint Declaration on the Doctrine of Justification, an official ecumenical document endorsed by the

Vatican in 1999 and created in collaboration with the Lutheran World Federation, says in paragraph seven, "... this declaration is shaped by the conviction that in their respective histories our churches have come to new insights."[7] These "new insights" include the realization of Trent's misguided critique of Protestant doctrines, such as justification by faith alone. This, it seems, is the view that guides the understanding of many contemporary Catholic theologians, particularly those with an ecumenical bent.

It is important to realize that many Catholics, including Pope (Emeritus) Benedict himself, don't understand justification in a rigidly Tridentine light.[8] For instance, in the pope's sermon on justification in Saint Peter's Square on November 19, 2008, he said, "Being just simply means being with Christ and in Christ. And this suffices. Further observances are no longer necessary. For this reason Luther's phrase: 'faith alone' is true, if it is not opposed to faith in charity in love."[9] A week later, on November 26 in the Paul VI Audience Hall, the pontiff continued this emphasis: "Following Saint Paul, we have seen that man is unable to 'justify' himself with his own actions, but can only truly become 'just' before God because God confers his 'justice' upon him, uniting him to Christ his Son. And man obtains this union through faith. In this sense, Saint Paul tells us: not our deeds, but rather faith renders us 'just.'"[10] Lest you think the pope's statements were an out-of-turn, momentary flash in the pan, you can also read them in his book *Saint Paul*.

Such verbal agreement concerning the phrase "faith

alone," however, should not be understood as equivalent to the understanding of Reformed Protestantism. With Trent, modern Catholicism is keen to ground justification in the faith that is formed by love in a sacramental framework beginning with baptism. Hence, the Catholic *Catechism* asserts: "The grace of the Holy Spirit confers upon us the righteousness of God. Uniting us by faith and Baptism to the Passion and Resurrection of Christ, the Spirit makes us sharers in his life."[11] Simply put, for Rome faith is "alone" over against relying upon one's human resources, but it is nevertheless always embedded in charity in the context of the sacramental life. In the final analysis, *sola fide* continues to be a point of genuine division between Catholics and Protestants.

Critical as it is for us to examine these historical and theological details, we can't stop here. We must probe further to consider how these implications relate to the enterprise of proclaiming Christ — the message of divine grace accessed through faith alone — into the hearts of Catholic people who are unaware of why Jesus died. Catholic philosopher Peter Kreeft describes this challenge:

> There are still many who do not know the data, the gospel. Most of my Catholic students at Boston College have never heard it. They do not even know how to get to heaven. When I ask them what they would say to God if they died tonight and God asked them why he should take them into heaven, nine out of ten do not even mention Jesus Christ. Most of them say they have been good or kind or sincere or did their

best. So I seriously doubt God will undo the Reformation until he sees to it that Luther's reminder of Paul's gospel has been heard throughout the church.[12]

This is where the rubber hits the road for our doctrine of justification by faith alone.

Question 5: Some of the reasons that Catholics say they convert to evangelical faith include a desire to be motivated by grace rather than guilt, or to have a relationship with Christ rather than a rules-based understanding of religion. Aren't there cases in evangelical circles where we make the same mistakes (emphasize guilt, rules, etc.)? If so, does this necessarily mean that Catholicism is invalidated by some of the mistaken practices of its adherents?

Indeed, we must recognize that Protestants are also guilty of legalism. Most of us have encountered ardent fundamentalists for whom law-keeping is the way of salvation. I think, however, there is probably a difference between Catholic and Protestant *teaching* on this point. When Protestant teachers use guilt as a motivation, they do so as a departure from biblical teaching. For the Catholic, however, motivation by guilt is to some degree an outworking of Catholic tradition. For instance, in the so-called precepts of the Catholic Church (i.e., abstaining from meat on Lenten Fridays, holy days of obligation, auricular confession) one is exhorted to observe various rituals as a way of maintaining his or her salvation.[13] The doctrine of purgatory also feeds the guilt tendency. For many, this results in a form of "salvation on probation."

Thus, guilt becomes a regular pattern that shapes how one understands God, self, and salvation.

Question 6: What can Evangelicals learn from their conversations with Catholic friends and families?

Let us begin by recognizing the assumption of this question: that Protestants *can* and *should* learn from Catholics. I think this assumption is right for two basic reasons. First, it is sophomoric at best to think that we have nothing to learn from other Christian traditions. When I was a student at Gordon-Conwell Theological Seminary, for instance, I took classes at other divinity schools in the Boston area. I studied Eastern Orthodoxy at Holy Cross and Roman Catholicism among Catholics from Boston College.[14] These classmates taught me profound lessons about reverence for God, prayer, bioethics, natural law, and social justice. These and other lessons we can learn from our Catholic friends and family. Did I agree with everything I heard from these classmates? No, yet their perspectives broadened and enriched mine. You say, "Well, my cousin Vito, the most outspoken member of my Catholic family, isn't exactly the Boston College type." Fair enough. But that brings me to the second reason why we must take the posture of a humble listener. It is essentially the law of reciprocity. If you and I ever hope to communicate effectively, we must first establish trust and credibility, currency that comes by listening before we talk. This approach, characterized by genuine concern, will enrich relationships and therefore promote fruitful conversation about the gospel.

Question 7: How can you clearly articulate some of the significant differences in doctrine between Evangelicals and Roman Catholics and yet continue to call Catholics "brothers and sisters in Christ"? For many of the Reformers, the doctrinal differences led to quite different conclusions about where Roman Catholics stand in their relationship with God. I am wondering if you can explore further what believing basic Catholic doctrine means for the average Catholic's relationship with God? How do we juggle the importance of calling on our Catholic friends to turn away from Catholic beliefs and practices that are in error with the reality that they already believe in God who is Father, Son, and Holy Spirit?

The Bible teaches that one must believe *with* faith alone (Rom. 4:4; Eph. 2:8 – 9; Titus 3:5), but it doesn't require that one believe *in* faith alone as a body of doctrine. John Piper makes this point when he quotes theologian John Owen, who wrote, " 'Men may be really saved by that grace which *doctrinally they do deny;* and they may be justified by the imputation of that righteousness which *in opinion they deny to be imputed.'* ... Owen's words are not meant to make us cavalier about the content of the gospel, but to hold out hope that men's hearts are often better than their heads."[15] According to Owen, some Catholics evidently appear to trust in Jesus alone for salvation, despite the teaching of their Church.

If this sounds anti-Catholic, please keep in mind that the Catholic Church has something similar to say about Protestants. From the Catholic point of view, the

Evangelical's hope in justification is mediated through baptism, which is thought to reflect the Catholic sacrament of baptism. We Protestants may think that we're justified by faith alone, says the Catholic, but it is actually on account of our baptism, which finds legitimacy in the Catholic sacrament. Am I offended by the Catholic view? No, because I realize it is not personal; Catholics are simply expressing the teaching of their Church with candor while seeking to grant legitimacy to me as a Protestant brother. Hopefully, my comments are read in the same spirit.

This question's reference to the Reformers is interesting. It is undoubtedly true that many of them regarded Catholics to be outside the pale of biblical teaching, yet not all of them did. In fact, there is a significant tradition in evangelical theology of those who regard Catholicism to be an orthodox expression of Christianity, even as we strongly disagree on issues of authority and the doctrine of salvation.

For all of the sharp invectives that Martin Luther launched against the papacy and clergy, he was not as harsh toward all Catholic *people*. This was so because under the layers of Catholic tradition, Luther recognized a scriptural core that could truly generate and nurture faith. In his words, "The Roman Church is holy, because it has God's holy name, the gospel, baptism, etc."[16]

Calvin expressed a similar sentiment in his letter to Cardinal Sadoleto, stating that despite serious differences of doctrine, "[it doesn't mean] that Roman Catholics are not also Christians. We indeed, Sadoleto, do not deny that those over which you preside are Churches of Christ."[17]

Over three hundred years later, in 1869, Princeton theologian Charles Hodge wrote to Pope Pius IX declining an invitation to attend Vatican I. After citing the reasons why his attendance and that of his delegates would not happen, he offers the following conclusion:

> Nevertheless, although we cannot return to the fellowship of the Church of Rome, we desire to live in charity with all men. We love all those who love our Lord Jesus Christ in sincerity.
>
> We regard as Christian brethren all who worship, love, and obey him as their God and Saviour, and we hope to be united in heaven with all who unite with us on earth in saying, "Unto him that loved us, and washed us from our sins in his own blood, and hath made us kings and priests unto God and his Father; to him be glory and dominion forever and ever. Amen" (Rev. 1:6).[18]

Finally, in addition to Hodge, we find this statement from another theologian of Princeton, J. Gresham Machen. Writing fifty years later about the relatively close proximity of Catholics to Evangelicals, compared to the chasm separating Evangelicals from liberals, Machen highlights our common ground:

> Yet how great is the common heritage that unites the Roman Catholic Church ... to devout Protestants today! [As significant as our difference is] ... it seems almost trifling compared to the abyss which stands between us and many ministers of our own church.[19]

This leads me to the final part of this question: "How do we juggle the importance of calling on our Roman Catholic friends to turn away from Roman Catholic beliefs and practices that are in error with the reality that they believe in God who is Father, Son, and Holy Spirit?"

I suggest that we follow the Protestant Reformers, and, more importantly, Jesus himself, by expressing honesty about where we differ, and, at the same time, extending brotherly love in our areas of agreement with Catholics. The primary biblical touchstone for this is John 1:14 where it is written of Jesus that he came "full of grace and truth." There you have it. That is the *how*. As our Lord maintained these virtues with a balanced poise, we seek to do the same. We can't justify behavior that is irritable and crotchety, certainly not on the basis of the Bible. On the other hand, we must not be so open-minded that our brains fall out of our heads; we must have the theological *chutzpah* to be honest.

When a Catholic confesses the gospel and lives for Jesus, I want to apply the love about which 1 Corinthians 13 speaks — love that "bears all things, believes all things, hopes all things" (NASB), a love that extends the benefit of the doubt, puts its arm around this Catholic friend, and calls him "brother." I'm also going to proclaim the gospel and extend discipleship so that I and my Catholic friend together realize a greater level of sanctification. Would I like to see this friend eventually leave the Catholic Church? Eventually, yes. I am a Protestant pastor who believes that on the issues of Christian authority and salvation Protestants are fundamentally right. To say otherwise would be disingenuous. And yet, I'm not going to insist that such a departure happen in *my* time frame. The Lord is my friend's shepherd as much as he is mine. Indeed, I must apply my doctrine of providence at this point by faithfully and winsomely trusting in God's sovereignly timed oversight. Thus, in the final analysis, we must approach this activity as Peter says in his first epistle, endeavoring to "honor Christ the Lord as holy, always being prepared to make a defense to anyone who asks you for a reason for the hope that is in you; yet do it with gentleness and respect" (1 Peter 3:15–16 ESV).

Question 8: If one's theology resembles that of Luther or Calvin, should we not also emulate their confrontational polemics (manner of argumentation)?

Concerning our rhetorical engagement with the Catholic Church, we must recognize that we live in a different time period from Luther and Calvin. In the twenty-first century we don't typically link Christian faith to physical violence (thankfully). However, it was far different in the sixteenth and seventeenth centuries when religious solidarity and national destiny went hand-in-hand. In such a society, the idea of religious pluralism was new and frightening. With what church does one identify? Even saying it this way is somewhat misleading. There was hardly a pluralistic choice. When Luther published his *Appeal to the German Nobility*, for instance, he was not proposing an alternative option. It was, for him, a necessary *replacement* of an apostate church institution. In addition to generating profound existential angst among rank-and-file Christians, such transition created a social and political revolution, which the wars of religion vividly remind us.

In this setting, words were employed to heighten concern, awaken emotions, and motivate action. In this clash of competing worldviews, where the stakes were life and death, rhetorical conventions permitted and even promoted an aggressive confrontation aimed at demeaning opponents. In this polemical universe, you could not punch below the belt, because there was no belt marking off acceptable and unacceptable blows. My friend Jason illustrated this point during seminary. The consummate Calvinist, Jason once mentioned nonchalantly to our classmate Linford, a Mennonite friend: "If we were living five hundred years ago, I'd be drowning you about now." The strength of their friendship allowed for such a bizarre statement. Perhaps the most bizarre part, however, was its truth.

With regard to polemics, we live in a new day. The influence of Christian virtue on verbal etiquette has delivered us from the violent vituperations of yesteryear. In other words, we can disagree with charity. This is not to say that the Reformation is therefore over. Far from it. The same fundamental issues of difference that separated Catholics and Protestants in the sixteenth century largely exist today. But instead of drowning or impaling our Catholic conversation partners, we may now enjoy a cup of coffee with them at Starbucks, pray for their families, and cherish them as friends.

This sort of humility doesn't mean that we have

compromised our conviction of what constitutes truth. Only after reaching an informed conviction, having taken time to listen, learn, and think, do we possess the requisite courage to relate to others in a vulnerable, humble way. Conversely, when we attack the jugular of the one who disagrees with us, we demonstrate our insecurity. Once again, Jesus is our example. Although God, Jesus did not exploit his deity, but made himself nothing, taking the form of a servant (Phil. 2:6–7).

Question 9: What is a lesson that you think Evangelicals should learn from the Catholic tradition?

I have heard Catholics say of evangelical Protestants: "You are so heavenly minded that you are no earthly good." This critique describes those who overlook the tangible needs of society because they are perceived to be outside the purview of Christian ministry. It is encapsulated in the words of a Protestant preacher who was purported as saying, "Don't carry a loaf of bread in one hand and the Bible in the other, lest in your efforts to feed the poor you forget that you're carrying the Word of God."

The Catholic tradition is especially poised to offer insight and provoke our thinking in this area. Growing out of its "incarnational" theology, Catholic ministry is often concerned with how the redemption of Christ addresses the practical needs of our world. Whether in the arena of education, politics, economics, sexual ethics, prison reform, poverty, race issues, or sanctity of life, Catholic tradition offers a robust moral theology that is deeper and fuller than the typical paradigm with which Protestants operate.

Having served as pastor of a church's community outreach ministry, I am aware of how we Evangelicals sometimes struggle with understanding how gospel outreach relates to the enterprise of cultural engagement. I readily affirm that the work of social justice must be properly distinguished from the activity of preaching the death and resurrection of Jesus. And I also believe that the Great Commission is first and foremost concerned with gospel outreach and discipleship. However, at the same time, it is appropriate for such "Word-centered" ministry to move along a trajectory that eventually impacts the tangible dimensions of life.

Thankfully, there is an awareness among Evangelicals today of the need to repent of our unbiblical dualisms. The late British pastor, John Stott, makes the point:

> It is exceedingly strange that any followers of Jesus Christ should ever have needed to ask whether social involvement was their concern, and that controversy should have blown up over the relationship between Evangelicalism and social responsibility. For it is evident that in his public ministry Jesus both "went about ... teaching ... and preaching" (Matt 4:23; 9:35 RSV) and "went about doing good and healing" (Acts 10:38 RSV). In consequence, evangelism and social concern have been intimately related to one another throughout the history of the Church.[20]

Question 10: Is religious dialogue with Catholics desirable?

To many evangelical Protestants the word "dialogue" is

akin to the word "ecumenism," which, in their lexicon, is another way of saying "theological compromise." These individuals fear that such discussion is simply a prelude to suppressing genuine differences in a lowest-common-denominator approach to unity. In fact, over the years I have noticed a fascinating phenomenon that bears this out. Very often, if I am speaking with a group on the subject of Catholicism and use the word "dialogue," it won't be long before someone raises a hand and asks me what I think of the ECT (Evangelicals and Catholics Together) document of 1994 (which many regard as having driven off the cliff of doctrinal compromise). It has happened so many times that I now anticipate it. The unspoken assumption is that *dialogue leads to a reduction of the gospel*.

The fact that some ecumenical discussions have laid claim to more consensus than actually exists should be a healthy caution, but it should not undermine the value of dialogue, for such occasions provide the opportunity to convey biblical truth and to recognize the implicit *concerns* of our Catholic friends. As mentioned earlier, the doctrine of justification is an outstanding example of how this works. Evangelical Protestants are keen to emphasize the redemptive grace and assurance that is accounted to everyone who believes in Christ. We do this to safeguard the gracious character of justification. Roman Catholics, concerned that a purely external righteousness will fail to promote actual holiness, stress the process of transformation in which the Holy Spirit renews the soul. Recognizing the existence of these concerns is invaluable to fruitful conversation. Tony Lane highlights two benefits that we receive as a result: "First, it can give one greater understanding of Catholic teaching and the realization that statements that one considers objectionable may nonetheless have been motivated by a concern that is legitimate, albeit misapplied. Secondly, an awareness of Catholic concerns can help Evangelicals to be more critical of their own teaching."[21]

Having participated in a small amount of formal dialogue with the Catholic Church's Pontifical Council for Promoting Christian Unity and informally among numerous Catholics, I believe that Lane's assessment is correct. We should not hesitate to dialogue with Catholic friends, learning from one another and celebrating areas of agreement, as long as we are also honest about our differences.

CONCLUSION

The challenge before us—applying grace and truth in gospel ministry—extends backward through the centuries. Its roots reach into the soil of the Garden of Eden where Adam and Eve consumed the forbidden fruit and found themselves in conflict with God and one another. Because their corruption is also our corruption, such conflict is inevitable.

Thankfully, God has not left us to die in the isolation of sin. On account of his unfathomable love, God sent his Son—the Prince of Peace. Christ came and died for us, the Lamb of God who reconciles us to the Father. And after three days of death, God raised him from the grave. This is the good news, which we receive by faith. Yes, we remain sinners even after conversion, but we are also saints, clothed in Christ's righteousness. By such grace, we bring eternal hope and healing to others, even those with whom we disagree.

God desires for his love to be reflected in our relationships with Catholics. It seems that many Protestants believe that in order to be a fervent and faithful Evangelical we must also be anti-Catholic. The preceding pages have argued that this notion is not only flawed but missionally disastrous for the way it undermines gospel outreach. Instead, we must take an approach that is defined by the Christian virtues of grace and truth — seriousness for biblical teaching and an equal measure of seriousness in loving others. Toward this end, I would like to conclude with a brief story that illustrates the point.

When my maternal grandfather died, I was asked to speak at his funeral service on Long Island, New York. The room was packed with my Catholic family and multitudes of friends. As I prepared to deliver the gospel, I thought deeply about how to effectively convey grace and truth. Thankfully, by this point I had come a long way from the evening when my friends and I offended Catholics in Chicago by preaching on the sidewalk of Holy Name Cathedral. By now I had already written my first book on Roman Catholicism. Nevertheless, this was shaping up to be a difficult situation.

Because my grandfather (to whom this book is dedicated) and I were extremely close, I preached with a measure of pathos that was noticeable. I also sought to be warm-hearted and sensitive. An acute feeling of loss coupled with the reality of death deepened my intensity, which culminated in an invitation to trust in Christ for salvation. And then there was silence. No one moved. Everyone simply stared at me. After several moments, it became awkward and I started to become unnerved. Another moment passed before Father Tom, my childhood priest, stood at the back of the room and proceeded to walk forward. Everyone's eyes followed him until he was directly before me. With a warm smile that I had come to know from early childhood, Father Tom exclaimed, "Christopher (you'll have to imagine the Long Island accent), what a fine message. This is precisely the good news that we need at a time like this. I am so proud of you and thankful for the way you have served your family."

What was going on here? Obviously, Father Tom read the situation. He recognized that virtually everyone in the room was Catholic, and that this Protestant pastor was experiencing a deficiency of honor in his hometown. Therefore, with kindness and compassion, he stepped forward to put his imprimatur on my message. Such an expression of love in the context of gospel proclamation offers a glimpse into the crucial balance that this book has sought to promote: Truth and grace. Honesty and humility. In applying these virtues we have the privilege of communicating to the world that Jesus Christ is Lord.

THE APOSTLES' CREED

I believe in God, the Father Almighty,
    the Maker of heaven and earth,
    and in Jesus Christ, His only Son, our Lord:
    Who was conceived by the Holy Ghost,
    born of the virgin Mary,
    suffered under Pontius Pilate,
    was crucified, dead, and buried;
    He descended into hell
    The third day He arose again from the dead;
    He ascended into heaven,
    and sitteth on the right hand of God the Father
        Almighty;
    from thence he shall come to judge the quick and
        the dead.
I believe in the Holy Ghost;
    the holy catholic church;
    the communion of saints;
    the forgiveness of sins;
    the resurrection of the body;
    and the life everlasting. Amen.

THE NICENE CREED

I believe in one God, the Father Almighty, Maker of heaven and earth, and of all things visible and invisible.

And in one Lord Jesus Christ, the only-begotten Son of God, begotten of the Father before all worlds; God of God, Light of Light, very God of very God; begotten, not made, being of one substance with the Father, by whom all things were made.

Who, for us men and for our salvation, came down from heaven, and was incarnate by the Holy Spirit of the virgin Mary, and was made man; and was crucified also for us under Pontius Pilate; He suffered and was buried; and the third day He rose again, according to the Scriptures; and ascended into heaven, and sits on the right hand of the Father; and He shall come again, with glory, to judge the quick and the dead; whose kingdom shall have no end.

And I believe in the Holy Ghost, the Lord and Giver of Life; who proceeds from the Father and the Son; who with the Father and the Son together is worshipped and glorified; who spoke by the prophets.

And I believe in one holy catholic and apostolic Church. I acknowledge one baptism for the remission of sins; and I look for the resurrection of the dead, and the life of the world to come. Amen.

THE LAUSANNE COVENANT

(1974)

INTRODUCTION

We, members of the Church of Jesus Christ, from more than 150 nations, participants in the International Congress on World Evangelization at Lausanne, praise God for his great salvation and rejoice in the fellowship he has given us with himself and with each other. We are deeply stirred by what God is doing in our day, moved to penitence by our failures and challenged by the unfinished task of evangelization. We believe the gospel is God's good news for the whole world, and we are determined by his grace to obey Christ's commission to proclaim it to all mankind and to make disciples of every nation. We desire, therefore, to affirm our faith and our resolve, and to make public our covenant.

1. THE PURPOSE OF GOD

We affirm our belief in the one-eternal God, Creator and Lord of the world, Father, Son and Holy Spirit, who governs all things according to the purpose of his will. He has been calling out from the world a people for himself, and sending his people back into the world to be his servants and his witnesses, for the extension of his kingdom, the building up of Christ's body, and the glory of his name. We confess with shame that we have often denied our calling and failed in our mission, by becoming conformed to the world or by withdrawing from it. Yet we rejoice that even when borne by earthen vessels the gospel is still a precious treasure. To the task of making that treasure known in the power of the Holy Spirit we desire to dedicate ourselves anew.

(Isa. 40:28; Matt. 28:19; Eph. 1:11; Acts 15:14; John 17:6, 18; Eph. 4:12; 1 Cor. 5:10; Rom. 12:2; 2 Cor. 4:7)

2. THE AUTHORITY AND POWER OF THE BIBLE

We affirm the divine inspiration, truthfulness and authority of both Old and New Testament Scriptures in their entirety as the only written word of God, without error in all that it affirms, and the only infallible rule of faith and practice. We also affirm the power of God's word to accomplish his purpose of salvation. The message of the Bible is addressed to all men and women. For God's revelation in Christ and in Scripture is unchangeable. Through it the Holy Spirit still speaks today. He illumines the minds of God's people in every culture to perceive its truth freshly through their own eyes and thus discloses to the whole Church ever more of the many-colored wisdom of God.

(2 Tim. 3:16; 2 Peter 1:21; John 10:35; Isa. 55:11; 1 Cor. 1:21; Rom. 1:16, Matt. 5:17, 18; Jude 3; Eph. 1:17, 18; 3:10, 18)

3. THE UNIQUENESS AND UNIVERSALITY OF CHRIST

We affirm that there is only one Savior and only one gospel, although there is a wide diversity of evangelistic approaches. We recognize that everyone has some knowledge of God through his general revelation in nature. But we deny that this can save, for people suppress the truth by their unrighteousness. We also reject as derogatory to Christ and the gospel every kind of syncretism and dialogue which implies that Christ speaks equally through all religions and ideologies. Jesus Christ, being himself the only God-man, who gave himself as the only ransom for sinners, is the only mediator between God and people. There is no other name by which we must be saved. All men and women are perishing because of sin, but God loves everyone, not wishing that any should perish but that all should repent. Yet those who reject Christ repudiate the joy of salvation and condemn themselves to eternal separation from God. To proclaim Jesus as "the Savior of the world" is not to affirm that all people are either automatically or ultimately saved, still less to affirm that all religions offer salvation in Christ. Rather it is to proclaim God's love for a world of sinners and to invite everyone to respond to him as Savior and Lord in the wholehearted personal commitment of repentance and faith. Jesus Christ has been exalted above every other name; we long for the day when every knee shall bow to him and every tongue shall confess him Lord.

(Gal. 1:6–9; Rom. 1:18–32; 1 Tim. 2:5, 6; Acts 4:12; John 3:16–19; 2 Peter 3:9; 2 Thess. 1:7–9; John 4:42; Matt. 11:28; Eph. 1:20, 21; Phil. 2:9–11)

4. THE NATURE OF EVANGELISM

To evangelize is to spread the good news that Jesus Christ died for our sins and was raised from the dead according to the Scriptures, and that as the reigning Lord he now offers the forgiveness of sins and the liberating gifts of the Spirit to all who repent and believe. Our Christian presence in the world is indispensable to evangelism, and so is that kind of dialogue whose purpose is to listen sensitively in order to understand. But evangelism itself is the proclamation of the historical, biblical Christ as Savior and Lord, with a view to persuading people to come to him personally and so be reconciled to God. In issuing the gospel invitation we have no liberty to conceal the cost of discipleship. Jesus still calls all who would follow him to deny themselves, take up their cross, and identify themselves with his new community. The results of evangelism include obedience to Christ, incorporation into his Church and responsible service in the world.

(1 Cor. 15:3, 4; Acts 2:32–39; John 20:21; 1 Cor. 1:23; 2 Cor. 4:5; 5:11, 20; Luke 14:25–33; Mark 8:34; Acts 2:40, 47; Mark 10:43–45)

5. CHRISTIAN SOCIAL RESPONSIBILITY

We affirm that God is both the Creator and the Judge of all people. We therefore should share his concern for justice and reconciliation throughout human society and for the liberation of men and women from every kind of oppression. Because men and women are made in the image of God, every person, regardless of race, religion, color, culture, class, sex or age, has an intrinsic dignity because of which he or she should be respected and served, not exploited. Here too we express penitence both for our neglect and for having sometimes regarded evangelism and social concern as mutually exclusive. Although reconciliation with other people is not reconciliation with God, nor is social action evangelism, nor is political liberation salvation, nevertheless we affirm that evangelism and socio-political involvement are both part of our Christian duty. For both are necessary expressions of our doctrines of God and man, our love for our neighbor and our obedience to Jesus Christ. The message of salvation implies also a message of judgment upon every form of alienation, oppression and discrimination, and we should not be afraid to denounce evil and injustice wherever they exist. When people receive Christ they are born again into his kingdom and must seek not only to exhibit but also to spread its righteousness in the midst of

TALKING WITH CATHOLICS ABOUT THE GOSPEL

an unrighteous world. The salvation we claim should be transforming us in the totality of our personal and social responsibilities. Faith without works is dead.

(Acts 17:26, 31; Gen. 18:25; Isa. 1:17; Ps. 45:7; Gen. 1:26, 27; James 3:9; Lev. 19:18; Luke 6:27, 35; James 2:14–26; John 3:3, 5; Matt. 5:20; 6:33; 2 Cor. 3:18; James 2:20)

6. THE CHURCH AND EVANGELISM

We affirm that Christ sends his redeemed people into the world as the Father sent him, and that this calls for a similar deep and costly penetration of the world. We need to break out of our ecclesiastical ghettos and permeate non-Christian society. In the Church's mission of sacrificial service evangelism is primary. World evangelization requires the whole Church to take the whole gospel to the whole world. The Church is at the very center of God's cosmic purpose and is his appointed means of spreading the gospel. But a church which preaches the cross must itself be marked by the cross. It becomes a stumbling block to evangelism when it betrays the gospel or lacks a living faith in God, a genuine love for people, or scrupulous honesty in all things including promotion and finance. The Church is the community of God's people rather than an institution, and must not be identified with any particular culture, social or political system, or human ideology.

(John 17:18; 20:21; Matt. 28:19, 20; Acts 1:8; 20:27; Eph. 1:9, 10; 3:9–11; Gal. 6:14, 17; 2 Cor. 6:3, 4; 2 Tim. 2:19–21; Phil. 1:27)

7. COOPERATION IN EVANGELISM

We affirm that the Church's visible unity in truth is God's purpose. Evangelism also summons us to unity, because our oneness strengthens our witness, just as our disunity undermines our gospel of reconciliation. We recognize, however, that organizational unity may take many forms and does not necessarily forward evangelism. Yet we who share the same biblical faith should be closely united in fellowship, work and witness. We confess that our testimony has sometimes been marred by a sinful individualism and needless duplication. We pledge ourselves to seek a deeper unity in truth, worship, holiness and mission. We urge the development of regional and functional cooperation for the furtherance of the Church's mission, for strategic planning, for mutual encouragement, and for the sharing of resources and experience.

(John 17:21, 23; Eph. 4:3, 4; John 13:35; Phil. 1:27; John 17:11–23)

8. CHURCHES IN EVANGELISTIC PARTNERSHIP

We rejoice that a new missionary era has dawned. The dominant role of western missions is fast disappearing. God is raising up from the younger churches a great new resource for world evangelization, and is thus demonstrating that the responsibility to evangelize belongs to the whole body of Christ. All churches should therefore be asking God and themselves what they should be doing both to reach their own area and to send missionaries to other parts of the world. A reevaluation of our missionary responsibility and role should be continuous. Thus a growing partnership of churches will develop and the universal character of Christ's Church will be more clearly exhibited. We also thank God for agencies which labor in Bible translation, theological education, the mass media, Christian literature, evangelism, missions, church renewal and other specialist fields. They too should engage in constant self-examination to evaluate their effectiveness as part of the Church's mission.

(Rom. 1:8; Phil. 1:5; 4:15; Acts 13:1–3, 1 Thess. 1:6–8)

9. THE URGENCY OF THE EVANGELISTIC TASK

More than 2,700 million people, which is more than two-thirds of all humanity, have yet to be evangelized. We are ashamed that so many have been neglected; it is a standing rebuke to us and to the whole Church. There is now, however, in many parts of the world an unprecedented receptivity to the Lord Jesus Christ. We are convinced that this is the time for churches and parachurch agencies to pray earnestly for the salvation of the unreached and to launch new efforts to achieve world evangelization. A reduction of foreign missionaries and money in an evangelized country may sometimes be necessary to facilitate the national church's growth in self-reliance and to release resources for unevangelized areas.

Missionaries should flow ever more freely from and to all six continents in a spirit of humble service. The goal should be, by all available means and at the earliest possible time, that every person will have the opportunity to hear, understand, and to receive the good news. We cannot hope to attain this goal without sacrifice. All of us are shocked by the poverty of millions and disturbed by the injustices which cause it. Those of us who live in affluent circumstances accept our duty to develop a simple life-style in order to contribute more generously to both relief and evangelism.

(John 9:4; Matt. 9:35–38; Rom. 9:1–3; 1 Cor. 9:19–23; Mark 16:15; Isa. 58:6, 7; James 1:27; 2:1–9; Matt. 25:31–46; Acts 2:44, 45; 4:34, 35)

10. EVANGELISM AND CULTURE

The development of strategies for world evangelization calls for imaginative pioneering methods. Under God, the result will be the rise of churches deeply rooted in Christ and closely related to their culture. Culture must always be tested and judged by Scripture. Because men and women are God's creatures, some of their culture is rich in beauty and goodness. Because they are fallen, all of it is tainted with sin and some of it is demonic. The gospel does not presuppose the superiority of any culture to another, but evaluates all cultures according to its own criteria of truth and righteousness, and insists on moral absolutes in every culture. Missions have all too frequently exported with the gospel an alien culture and churches have sometimes been in bondage to culture rather than to Scripture. Christ's evangelists must humbly seek to empty themselves of all but their personal authenticity in order to become the servants of others, and churches must seek to transform and enrich culture, all for the glory of God.

(Mark 7:8, 9, 13; Gen. 4:21, 22; 1 Cor. 9:19–23; Phil. 2:5–7; 2 Cor. 4:5)

11. EDUCATION AND LEADERSHIP

We confess that we have sometimes pursued church growth at the expense of church depth, and divorced evangelism from Christian nurture. We also acknowledge that some of our missions have been too slow to equip and encourage national leaders to assume their rightful responsibilities. Yet we are committed to indigenous principles, and long that every church will have national leaders who manifest a Christian style of leadership in terms not of domination but of service. We recognize that there is a great need to improve theological education, especially for church leaders. In every nation and culture there should be an effective training program for pastors and laity in doctrine, discipleship, evangelism, nurture and service. Such training programs should not rely on any stereotyped methodology but should be developed by creative local initiatives according to biblical standards.

(Col. 1:27, 28; Acts 14:23; Titus 1:5, 9; Mark 10:42–45; Eph. 4:11, 12)

12. SPIRITUAL CONFLICT

We believe that we are engaged in constant spiritual warfare with the principalities and powers of evil, who are seeking to overthrow the Church and frustrate its task of world evangelization. We know our need to equip ourselves with God's armor and to fight this battle with the spiritual weapons of truth and prayer. For we detect the activity of our enemy, not only in false ideologies outside the Church, but also inside it in false gospels which twist Scripture and put people in the place of God. We need both watchfulness and discernment to safeguard the biblical gospel. We acknowledge that we ourselves are not immune to worldliness of thoughts and action, that is, to a surrender to secularism. For example, although careful studies of church growth, both numerical and spiritual, are right and valuable, we have sometimes neglected them. At other times, desirous to ensure a response to the gospel, we have compromised our message, manipulated our hearers through pressure techniques, and become unduly preoccupied with statistics or even dishonest in our use of them. All this is worldly. The Church must be in the world; the world must not be in the Church.

(Eph. 6:12; 2 Cor. 4:3, 4; Eph. 6:11, 13–18; 2 Cor. 10:3–5; 1 John 2:18–26; 4:1–3; Gal. 1:6–9; 2 Cor. 2:17; 4:2; John 17:15)

13. FREEDOM AND PERSECUTION

It is the God-appointed duty of every government to secure conditions of peace, justice and liberty in which the Church may obey God, serve the Lord Jesus Christ, and preach the gospel without interference. We therefore pray for the leaders of nations and call upon them to guarantee freedom of thought and conscience, and freedom to practice and propagate religion in accordance with the will of God and as set forth in The Universal Declaration of Human Rights. We also express our deep concern for all who have been unjustly imprisoned, and especially for those who are suffering for their testimony to the Lord Jesus. We promise to pray and work for their freedom. At the same time we refuse to be intimidated by their fate. God helping us, we too will seek to stand against injustice and to remain faithful to the gospel, whatever the cost. We do not forget the warnings of Jesus that persecution is inevitable.

(1 Tim. 1:1–4; Acts 4:19; 5:29; Col. 3:24; Heb. 13:1–3; Luke 4:18; Gal. 5:11; 6:12; Matt. 5:10–12; John 15:18–21)

14. THE POWER OF THE HOLY SPIRIT

We believe in the power of the Holy Spirit. The Father sent his Spirit to bear witness to his Son; without his witness ours is futile. Conviction of sin, faith in Christ, new birth and Christian growth are all his work. Further, the Holy Spirit is a missionary spirit; thus evangelism should arise spontaneously from a Spirit-filled church. A church that is not a missionary church is contradicting itself and quenching the Spirit. Worldwide evangelization will become a realistic possibility only when the Spirit renews the Church in truth and wisdom, faith, holiness, love and power. We therefore call upon all Christians to pray for such a visitation of the sovereign Spirit of God that all his fruit may appear in all his people and that all his gifts may enrich the body of Christ. Only then will the whole church become a fit instrument in his hands, that the whole earth may hear his voice.

(1 Cor. 2:4; John 15:26, 27; 16:8–11; 1 Cor. 12:3; John 3:6–8; 2 Cor. 3:18; John 7:37–39; 1 Thess. 5:19; Acts 1:8; Ps. 85:4–7; 67:1–3; Gal. 5:22, 23; 1 Cor. 12:4–31; Rom. 12:3–8)

15. THE RETURN OF CHRIST

We believe that Jesus Christ will return personally and visibly, in power and glory, to consummate his salvation and his judgment. This promise of his coming is a further spur to our evangelism, for we remember his words that the gospel must first be preached to all nations. We believe that the interim period between Christ's ascension and return is to be filled with the mission of the people of God, who have no liberty to stop before the end. We also remember his warning that false Christs and false prophets will arise as precursors of the final Antichrist. We therefore reject as a proud, self-confident dream the notion that people can ever build a utopia on earth. Our Christian confidence is that God will perfect his kingdom, and we look forward with eager anticipation to that day, and to the new heaven and earth in which righteousness will dwell and God will reign forever. Meanwhile, we rededicate ourselves to the service of Christ and of people in joyful submission to his authority over the whole of our lives.

(Mark 14:62; Heb. 9:28; Mark 13:10; Acts 1:8–11; Matt. 28:20; Mark 13:21–23; 1 John 2:18; 4:1–3; Luke 12:32; Rev. 21:1–5; 2 Peter 3:13; Matt. 28:18)

CONCLUSION

Therefore, in the light of this our faith and our resolve, we enter into a solemn covenant with God and with each other, to pray, to plan and to work together for the evangelization of the whole world. We call upon others to join us. May God help us by his grace and for his glory to be faithful to this our covenant! Amen, Alleluia!

NOTES

INTRODUCTION

1. Chapter two provides a definition of the term "evangelical."
2. This analogy to Athenian pagans breaks down to the extent that our Catholic friends have embraced Christian truth.
3. 1 Corinthians 13:1 ESV.

CHAPTER TWO: UNDERSTANDING CATHOLICS

1. David Bebbington, *Evangelicalism in Modern Britain: A History from the 1730s to the 1980s* (London: Unwin Hyman, 1989).
2. See *The Advent of Evangelicalism: Exploring Historical Continuities*, eds. Michael Haykin and Kenneth Steward (Nashville: Broadman and Holman, 2008).
3. Elisabeth Jay, *The Evangelical and Oxford Movements* (Cambridge: Cambridge University Press, 1983), 1–19.
4. Ibid., 3.
5. Bebbington, *Evangelicalism in Modern Britain*, 1–19.
6. David Newsome, *The Parting of Friends: The Wilberforces and Henry Manning* (London: Eerdmans Publishing Co., 1966), 1–16.
7. Sheridan Gilley, *Newman and His Age* (Westminster: Christian Classics, 1991), 47–53.
8. David Bebbington has summarized evangelical religion in terms of his so-called quadrilateral: conversionism, activism, biblicism, crucicentrism. David Newsome and Sheridan Gilley identify common evangelical traits such as denominational secessions, biblical literalism, chiliasm, and social justice (Newsome, *The Parting*; Gilley, *Newman*). Elisabeth Jay distinguishes between "essential" and

"non-essential" features in her work, *The Religion of the Heart: Angli-can Evangelicalism and the Nineteenth-Century Novel* (Oxford: Clar-endon Press 1979), 51–105.

9. John Newton and Richard Cecil, *Out of the Depths: The Autobiogra-phy of John Newton*, 2nd ed. (London: C. J. Thynne & Jarvis, 1925).

10. For a history on each of these publications, see Peter Toon, *Evangeli-cal Theology* (St. Andrew: St. Andrew Press, 1979) 6–9.

11. Stephen Neill, *A History of Christian Missions*, 2nd ed. (Middlesex: Harmondsworth, 1986), 213–216.

12. John Henry Overton, *The Evangelical Revival in the Eighteenth Century* (London: Longmans, Green, 1886); J. C. Ryle, *Knots Untied: Being Plain Statements on Disputed Points in Religion from the Standpoint of an Evangelical Churchman* (London: National Protestant Church Union, 1898); H. C. G. Moule, *The Evangelical School in the Church of England: Its Men and Its Work in the Nineteenth Century* (London: J. Nisbet & Co., 1901); William Law Mathieson, *England in Transition, 1789–1832: A Study of Movements* (London: Longmans, Green, and Co. 1920); William Law Mathieson, *English Church Reform 1815–1840* (London: Longmans, Green and Co., 1923); Charles Smyth, *Simeon and Church Order: A Study of the Origins of the Evangelical Revival in Cambridge in the Eighteenth Century* (Cambridge: Cambridge Univer-sity Press, 1940); J. S. Reynolds, *The Evangelicals at Oxford, 1735–1871: A Record of an Unchronicled Movement with the Record Extended to 1905* (Oxford: Marcham Manor Press, 1975); Toon, *Evangelical Theology*; Jay, *The Evangelical and Oxford Movements*; Bebbington, *Evangelicalism*.

13. Ryle, *Knots Untied*, 3.

14. Ryle doesn't identify these individuals by name. Despite the "low church" origins of the movement, with its emphasis on Scripture only, priesthood of believers, and a general chilliness toward reli-gious "tradition," Ryle conveys his indebtedness to "the Thirty-nine Articles, the Prayer-book fairly interpreted, the works of the Reform-ers, [and] the writings of the pre-Caroline divines" (v).

15. Ryle, *Knots Untied*, 4–9.

16. George William Erskine Russell, *The Household of Faith: Portraits and Essays* (London: Hodder and Stoughton, 1902), 240.

17. Ibid.

18. It should be noted that "Evangelicalism" is a global movement that transcends the British and American story that we have told here. Philip Jenkins provides helpful insight into this scope in his work *The Next Christendom: The Coming of Global Christianity*, 3rd ed. (New York: Oxford University Press, 2011).

19. For more on this, see George Weigel, *Evangelical Catholicism: Deep*

Reform in the 21st-Century Church (New York: Basic Books, 2013). While this Catholic movement is outside of "Evangelicalism," properly speaking (following Bebbington's proposal, which limits the movement to Protestantism), Weigel develops familiar themes for his readers such as personal Bible reading, an emphasis on the new birth, and missional outreach.

20. Peter Feuerherd, *Holyland USA: A Catholic Ride through America's Evangelical Landscape* (New York: Crossroad Publishing, 2006), 72.
21. *Evangelical Catholicism*, 54–55.
22. Pope Paul VI, "Evangelii Nuntiandi," *The Vatican*, http://www.vatican.va/holy_father/paul_vi/apost_exhortations/documents/hf_pvi_exh_19751208_evangelii-nuntiandi_en.html (accessed July 24, 2014).
23. Ted Kennedy, *True Compass: A Memoir* (New York: Hachette, 2009), 29.
24. William V. D'Antonio, "New Survey Offers Portrait of U.S. Catholics," *National Catholic Reporter*, October 24, 2011, http://ncronline.org/news/catholics-america/persistence-and-change (accessed February 26, 2014).
25. "Evangelicals" are here defined as Protestant Christians who agree with the "Basis of Faith" of the European Evangelical Alliance. Used with permission from James Hatcher. This taxonomy also appears in my book, *Holy Ground: Walking with Jesus as a Former Catholic* (Grand Rapids: Zondervan, 2009), 164–166.
26. Jonathan Edwards, *The Nature of Virtue* (Ann Arbor: University of Michigan Press, 1960), 14–26.
27. Augustine, *The Trinity*, trans. Edmund Hill, ed. John E. Rotelle (Brooklyn: New City Press, 1991), books 8–9.

CHAPTER THREE: CATHOLIC HISTORY
SINCE THE SIXTEENTH CENTURY

1. So David Steimetz asserts, "It is important to remember that the Reformation began as an intra-Catholic debate." "The Intellectual Appeal of the Reformation," *Theology Today* 57 (2001) 459–472 (459).
2. Diarmaid MacCulloch is correct to caution against using the word "Protestant" as a simple description for "sympathizers with reform in the first half of the sixteenth century." He prefers the word "evangelical" as a more indicative term for the actual movement. "Evangelical," says MacCulloch, indicated the content of their belief and also the nomenclature of the period. *The Reformation: A History* (New York: Viking, 2003), xviii.

3. Eva-Marie Jung, "On the Nature of Evangelism in Sixteenth-Century Italy," *Journal of the History of Ideas* 14 (1953): 511–527 (513).

4. Oddone Ortolani, "The Hopes of the Italian Reformers in Roman Action," in *Italian Reformation Studies in Honor of Laelius Socinus*, ed. John A. Tedeschi (Florence: Felice Le Monnier, 1965), 13.

5. In addition to making a mockery of Christian piety, most popes of this era lacked the spiritual fortitude to implement genuine renewal. These spiritually malnourished popes included Pope Sixtus IV (1471–1484), Innocent VIII (1484–1492), Alexander VI (1492–1503), Pius III (1503), Julius II (1503–1513), Leo X (1513–1521), and Clement VII (1523–1534). Adrian XI (1522–1523) was a short-lived exception to this pattern. Their inability to instill confidence among the faithful inevitably promoted a movement of dissent.

6. Founded by Gaetano di Thiene (1480–1547), this group was established as an official order by Pope Clement VII in 1524 by the papal bull, *Exponi nobis*. Members of this group included Gian Matteo Giberti (later Cardinal-bishop of Verona), Jacopo Sadoleto (Cardinal-bishop of Carpentras, France), and Gianpetro Caraffa (Cardinal-bishop of Naples, later Pope Paul IV, prominent *zelanti* leader and catalyst of the Italian Inquisition). Frederic Church, *The Italian Reformers, 1534–1564* (New York: Columbia University Press, 1932; reprint, 1974), 21–22.

7. Founded by Antonio Maria Zaccaria (1502–1547) et al., the order was accepted by Clement VII in 1533 before Pope Paul III officially recognized them in 1535. Michael A. Mullett, *The Catholic Reformation* (London: Routledge, 1999), 73.

8. Steven E. Ozment, *The Age of Reform, 1250–1550: An Intellectual and Religious History of Late Medieval and Reformation Europe* (New Haven: Yale University Press, 1980), 404. The Discalced Carmelites and Society of Jesus also emerged during this era. While originating in Spain, their influence quickly traveled to Italy. The "Discalced" Carmelites ("without shoes," actually, they wore sandals) was a women's movement led by St. Teresa Avila (1515–1582). Teresa influenced St. John of the Cross (1542–1591) to found the first monastery of Discalced Carmelite Friars. Keith J. Egan, "The Spirituality of the Carmelites," in *Christian Spirituality: High Middle Ages and Reformation*, ed. Jill Raitt, Bernard McGinn, and John Meyendorff (London: Routledge & Kegan Paul, 1987), 50–62. For a helpful overview of the Jesuits during this period, see John W. O'Malley, *The First Jesuits* (Cambridge: Harvard University Press, 1993).

9. Notable (clerical) members of the *Spirituali* were Cardinal Gasparo Contarini, Cardinal Reginald Pole, Cardinal Giacomo Sadoleto,

Cardinal Giovanni Morone, Abbot Gregorio Cortese of San Georgio in Venice, Tommaso Badia (Master of the sacred palace), Bishop Gian Matteo Giberti of Verona, and Archbishop Federico Fregoso of Salerno. Background on each of these men is found in Church, *The Italian Reformers, 1534–1564*.

10. John T. Paoletti and Gary M. Radke, *Art in Renaissance Italy* (New York: Harry N. Abrams, 1997), 404. In his book *Michelangelo: A Tormented Life*, Antonio Forcellino also contends that Michelangelo was a member of the *Spirituali*; trans. Allan Cameron (Cambridge: Polity Press, 2009), 8.

11. In the words of Trent, "Our lord Jesus Christ, the son of God, first proclaimed with his own lips this gospel, which had in the past been promised by the prophets in the sacred scriptures; then he bade it preached to every creature through his apostles as the source of the whole truth of salvation and rule of conduct. The council clearly perceives that this truth and rule are contained in written books and in unwritten traditions which were received by the apostles from the mouth of Christ himself, or else have come down to us, handed on as it were from the apostles themselves at the inspiration of the holy Spirit." Norman P. Tanner, ed., *Decrees of the Ecumenical Councils*, 2 vols. (London: Sheed & Ward and Washington, D.C.: Georgetown University Press, 1990), 663.

12. Chapter seven of the Decree on Justification explains "what the justification of the sinner is and what are its causes." *Decrees of the Ecumenical Councils*, 673.

13. Thomas Bokenkotter, *A Concise History of the Catholic Church* (New York: Doubleday, 2004), 250–251.

14. Of course, naturalism became a threat to all churches, not simply the Catholic Church.

15. Bruce Shelley, *Church History in Plain Language*, 2nd ed. (Dallas: Word Publishers, 1995), 357.

16. Stephen Tomkins, *A Short History of Christianity* (Grand Rapids: Eerdmans, 2005), 205.

17. Shelley, *Church History in Plain Language*, 2nd ed., 359.

18. *Decrees of the Ecumenical Councils*, 816.

19. David Gibson, *The Coming Catholic Church: How the Faithful Are Shaping a New American Catholicism* (San Francisco: Harper, 2003), 48.

20. George Weigel, *Evangelical Catholicism: Deep Reform in the 21st-Century Church* (New York: Basic Books, 2013), 2, 9.

21. The Hail Mary is a form of devotion in which five or fifteen decades of Hail Marys are repeated, each preceded by an "Our Father" and followed by a "Glory Be."

22. *Rerum Novarum*, para. 3.

23. Ibid., para. 22.

24. These seven themes of Catholic social teaching are outlined by the United States Conference of Catholic Bishops, http://usccb.org/beliefs-and-teachings/what-we-believe/catholic-social-teaching/seven-themes-of-catholic-social-teaching.cfm (accessed January 3, 2014).

25. I highly recommend Thomas Cahill's biography titled *Pope John XXIII: A Life* (New York: Penguin, 2008).

26. George Weigel, *The End and the Beginning: Pope John Paul II—The Victory of Freedom, the Last Years, the Legacy* (New York: Doubleday, 2010), 458.

27. Shelley, *Church History in Plain Language*, 2nd ed., 452–453.

28. In Vatican II's own words: "Christ summons the Church to continual reformation as she sojourns here on earth. The Church is always in need of this, in so far as she is an institution of men here on earth. Thus if, in various times and circumstances, there have been deficiencies in moral conduct or in church discipline, or even in the way that church teaching has been formulated—to be carefully distinguished from the deposit of faith itself—these can and should be set right at the opportune moment" (*Decree on Ecumenism*, 6).

29. In the words of Pope John XXIII, the council would be "predominantly pastoral in character." Ralph M. Wiltgen, *The Rhine Flows into the Tiber* (Devon: Augustine Publishing Company, 1978), 15.

30. Mark Noll, *Turning Points: Decisive Moments in the History of Christianity* (Grand Rapids: Baker, 2001), 302.

31. Ibid.

32. Wiltgen, *The Rhine Flows into the Tiber*, 28.

33. Ibid., 28–29.

34. Scripture *and* tradition, asserted Trent (Session 4.8; April 8, 1546), were to be embraced as two equally authoritative sources of divine revelation. At Vatican II, four hundred years later, Rome emphasized that Scripture and tradition flow from the same divine wellspring, merge into a unity and move toward the same goal (*Dogmatic Constitution on Divine Revelation* 9, November 18, 1865; see also *Catechism of the Catholic Church*, 2nd ed., para. 80).

35. Shelley, *Church History in Plain Language*, 2nd ed., 457.

36. Catholic theology maintains that God created sexual intercourse to be unitive and procreative. Therefore, the Church considers the deliberate altering of fertility with the intention of preventing procreation to be sinful. Certain Natural Family Planning (NFP) methods are approved by the Church, such as the "Rhythm Method."

37. "Amid all the upheaval, the Church experienced a major exodus of priests, brothers, and nuns. From 1962 to 1974 the total number of seminarians in the United States alone decreased by 31 percent; and

between 1966 and 1972 nearly 8,000 American priests left the public ministry." Shelley, *Church History in Plain Language*, 2nd ed., 459.

38. Ralph M. McInerny, *What Went Wrong with Vatican II: The Catholic Crisis* (Manchester: Sophia Institute Press, 1998), 59–60.

39. Ibid., 60.

40. Ibid., 64. This statement is misleading. The Vatican II document titled *Lumen Gentium* affirms the binding authority of papal encyclicals when it says: "This religious submission of mind and will must be shown in a special way to the authentic magisterium of the Roman Pontiff, even when he is not speaking *ex cathedra*; that is, it must be shown in such a way that his supreme magisterium is acknowledged with reverence, the judgments made by him are sincerely adhered to, according to his manifest mind and will. His mind and will in the matter may be known either from the character of the documents, from his frequent repetition of the same doctrine, or from his manner of speaking" (*Lumen Gentium*, no. 25).

41. McInerny, *What Went Wrong with Vatican II*, 64.

42. Ibid.

43. Ibid., 65.

44. George Weigel, *Witness to Hope: The Biography of Pope John Paul II* (New York: HarperCollins, 1999), 342.

CHAPTER FOUR: SIMILARITIES AND DIFFERENCES BETWEEN CATHOLICS AND PROTESTANTS

1. Catholics and Protestants share a common Bible, notwithstanding the so-called Old Testament Apocrypha (or, in Catholic terms, the "Deuterocanonicals"). These are a collection of writings found in the Catholic Old Testament from the intertestamental period (the four hundred years between the Old and New Testaments), comprising seven books: Tobit, Judith, 1 Maccabees, 2 Maccabees, Wisdom of Solomon, Sirach (also called Ecclesiasticus), and Baruch. In addition, there are also passages of text: the Letter to Jeremiah (which became Baruch ch. 6), the Prayer of Azariah (which became Daniel 3:24–90), an additional 107 verses in the book of Esther, Susanna (which became Daniel 13), and Bel and the Dragon (which became Daniel 14). These books were made an official part of the Catholic Old Testament at the Council of Trent (1545–1563). Our New Testament canons are synonymous.

2. Our agreement on these subjects is meaningful and substantive even though it is imperfect.

3. The Magisterium is defined by the catechism as follows: "The living teaching office of the Church, whose task it is to give as authentic

interpretation of the word of God, whether in its written form (Sacred Scripture), or in the form of Tradition. The magisterium ensures the Church's fidelity to the teaching of the Apostles in matters of faith and morals" (*Catechism of the Catholic Church*, para. 85, 890, 2033; Avery Cardinal Dulles, "The Freedom of Theology," in *First Things*, May 2008, no. 183, 20).

4. Chapter seven of the Decree on Justification explains "what the justification of the sinner is and what are its causes." *Decrees of the Ecumenical Councils*, ed. Norman P. Tanner, vol. 2 (London: Sheed & Ward, 1990), 673.

5. This story has been reworked from my book, *Holy Ground: Walking with Jesus as a Former Catholic* (Grand Rapids: Zondervan, 1999), 59–61.

6. *Catechism of the Catholic Church*, para. 779. Emphasis added.

7. Ibid., para. 780.

8. Sebastian Tromp, S.J., *Corpus Christi Quod Est Ecclesia*, trans. Ann Condit (New York: Vantage, 1960), 194.

9. Pope Benedict XVI, Joseph Ratzinger, in *Communio: Vol. 1, The Unity of the Church* (Grand Rapids: Eerdmans, 2010), 73–74. Since Vatican II, the language of "Continuous Incarnation" has been eclipsed by the council's emphasis on "The Pilgrim People of God." Nevertheless, the incarnation concept is so fundamental that it is still helpful for understanding how Catholic authority operates.

10. So Calvin writes, "Therefore, the joining together of Head and members, that indwelling of Christ in our hearts—in short, that mystical union—are accorded by us the highest degree of importance" (*Institutes*, 3.11.10). For Calvin, solidarity with Christ is always the work of the Holy Spirit who unifies us to Christ.

11. Richard John Neuhaus, "The Catholic Difference," in *Evangelicals and Catholics Together: Toward a Common Mission*, ed. Charles Colson and Richard John Neuhaus (Dallas: Word Publishing, 1995), 216.

12. *Catechism of the Catholic Church*, para. 795.

13. Joseph Cardinal Ratzinger, *Principles of Catholic Theology: Building Stones for Fundamental Theology*, trans. Sr. Mary Frances McCarthy, S.N.D. (San Francisco: Ignatius, 1987), 44–47, 245. Some works that draw on this theme are Henri de Lubac, S.J., *Catholicism: A Study of Dogma in Relation to the Corporate Destiny of Mankind*, trans. Lancelot C. Sheppard (London: Burns, Oates & Washbourne, 1950); David Tracy, *The Analogical Imagination: Christian Theology and the Culture of Pluralism* (New York: Basic, 1977); and Sebastian Tromp, S.J. *Corpus Christi Quaod Est Ecclesia*, trans. Ann Condit (New York: Vantage, 1960).

14. *Catechism of the Catholic Church*, para. 97.
15. Apostolic Constitution of Pope Pius XII, *Munificentissimus Deus*, 11.
16. Ibid., 12.
17. Ibid.
18. In Augustine's words, "This grace hid itself under a veil in the Old Testament, but it has been revealed in the New Testament according to the most perfectly ordered dispensation of the ages." *Anti-Pelagian Writings*, ch. 27.
19. Two helpful works on the Magisterium include Francis A. Sullivan, *Magisterium: Teaching Authority in the Catholic Church* (New York: Paulist Press, 1983); and Avery Cardinal Dulles, *Magisterium: Teacher and Guardian of the Faith* (Naples: Sapientia Press, 2007).
20. Avery Cardinal Dulles, *Magisterium: Teacher and Guardian of the Faith*, 4.
21. *Dei Verbum*, 10.
22. Evangelicals make this case in a variety of ways. For instance, Mark Saucy uses the *munus triplex Christi* (the threefold office of Christ as prophet, priest, and king) to explain how the grounding of sacramental ecclesiology and soteriology is a misappropriation of incarnation theology. See Saucy, "Evangelicals, Catholics, and Orthodox Together: Is the Church the Extension of the Incarnation?" *JETS* 43 (2000): 193–212. In the vein of biblical theology is the work of Leonardo De Chirico, who compares the biblical adverbs *hapax* (a punctiliar event) and *mallon* (a continuous process) in light of Jesus' ascension to suggest that the Catholic emphasis on Christological continuation confuses redemptive historical time distinctions. See De Chirico, "The Blurring of Time Distinctions in Roman Catholicism," *Themelios* 29 (2004): 40–46. Similar to this is Herman Ridderbos's evaluation of Paul's "head" and "body" metaphors, the discontinuity of which, he argues, militates against the Catholic position. See Ridderbos, *Paul: An Outline of His Theology*, trans. John Richard De Witt (Grand Rapids: Eerdmans, 1975), 362–393. Kevin Vanhoozer's canonical linguistic approach is also illuminating, particularly as it differentiates the canonical script from the faith community. See Vanhoozer, *The Drama of Doctrine: A Canonical Linguistic Approach to Christian Theology* (Louisville: Westminster John Knox, 2005). For a classic Reformed defense of *sola scriptura* against the backdrop of Catholicism, see Herman Bavinck, *Reformed Dogmatics: Prolegomena*, vol. 1, ed. John Bolt, trans. John Vriend (Grand Rapids: Baker, 2003), 457ff.
23. The word "supreme" here is not to suggest that Scripture is superior to the person of Jesus. Rather, Scripture reveals the truth of Jesus in written form and thus bears witness to his supremacy. For one of the more readable and insightful explanations of the doctrine of

Scripture alone, see Keith A. Mathison, *The Shape of Sola Scriptura* (Moscow, Idaho: Canon, 2001).

24. John 1:1; cf. 1 Peter 1:23–25; 1 John 1:1; Rev. 19:13.

25. Alister McGrath, *Christianity's Dangerous Idea: The Protestant Revolution—A History from the Sixteenth Century to the Twenty-First* (New York: Harper Collins, 2007), 201.

26. *Catechism of the Catholic Church*, para. 888–892.

27. R. C. Sproul includes a copy of the Chicago Statement on Biblical Inerrancy in his book *Scripture Alone: The Evangelical Doctrine* (Phillipsburg, N.J.: P&R Publishing, 2005), 177–193. This particular quote is found on pages 189–190.

28. Augustine, *De Doctrina Christiana*, 2.6.7. Augustine explores challenges of interpreting obscure passages in several chapters of Book II and into Book III.

29. A. N. S. Lane, "Sola Scriptura? Making Sense of a Post-Reformation Slogan," in *A Pathway into the Holy Scriptures*, ed. D. F. Wright and Philip Satterthwaite (Grand Rapids: Eerdmans, 1994), 324.

30. This story has been reworked from my book, *Holy Ground: Walking with Jesus as a Former Catholic* (Grand Rapids: Zondervan, 1999), 119–120.

31. *Catechism of the Catholic Church*, para. 2010.

32. See the Vatican II document titled *Constitution on the Sacred Liturgy*. The word "perpetuated" is used in paragraph 47 (continue to 58 for the entire section). You'll also find the concept of eucharistic sacrifice in paragraphs 7, 8, and 83. Walter M. Abbott, S.J., ed., *The Documents of Vatican II* (New York: Herder and Herder, 1966). The current *Catechism of the Catholic Church* also conveys the idea in paragraphs 1371, 1372, 1410, and 1419. The eucharistic sacrifice is also applied to those who are in purgatory, para. 1371.

33. *Catechism of the Catholic Church*, para. 1367. See also paragraphs 1407–1410 and *Constitution on the Sacred Liturgy*, para. 48ff. A particularly clear explanation is found in Ralph Martin, *The Catholic Church at the End of an Age: What Is the Spirit Saying?* (San Francisco: Ignatius, 1994), 167–172.

34. Because of this punitive element, some have described purgatory as an exceedingly hot penalty box, albeit one that occurs after the game is over.

35. A primary reason why Protestants reject the doctrine of purgatory is that it denies the sufficiency of Christ's atoning death. According to the writer of Hebrews, "For by one offering [Jesus Christ] has made perfect forever those who are being made holy" (Heb. 10:14). Indeed, Jesus himself exclaimed from the cross, "It is finished" (John 19:30).

From such texts, Evangelicals assert that it is not purgation *after* the cross; it is purgation *of* the cross that makes us acceptable to God.

36. *Catechism of the Catholic Church*, para. 1988–1995.
37. Ibid., para. 1992.
38. Ibid., para. 2006–2011.
39. Ibid., para. 2010.
40. As John the apostle states, "Yet to all who did receive him [Jesus], to those who believed in his name, he gave the right to become children of God" (John 1:12).

CHAPTER FIVE: EMBODYING AND PROCLAIMING THE GOSPEL

1. We recognize, once again, that not all evangelical Protestants endorse the doctrine of eternal security. But even among those who don't (such as the Wesleyan tradition), there is generally a much firmer commitment to assurance than what we commonly find among our Catholic friends.
2. Anthony N. S. Lane, *Justification by Faith in Catholic-Protestant Dialogue: An Evangelical Assessment* (London: T&T Clark, 2002), 132–133.
3. Matthew 22:37–39.
4. Quoted by Timothy George, "Evangelicals and the Great Tradition," *First Things*, no. 175 (August/September 2007), 21.
5. Deuteronomy 4:24.
6. Annie Dillard, *Teaching a Stone to Talk* (New York: Harper and Row, 1982), 40–41.

CHAPTER SIX: THE TOP TEN QUESTIONS ABOUT CATHOLICISM

1. The final words of William Shakespeare's *Romeo and Juliet*, Act 5, Scene 3.
2. Philip Ryken, *My Father's World: Meditations on Christianity and Culture.* (Phillipsburg, N.J.: P&R Publishing, 2002), 230–231.
3. *Catechism of the Catholic Church*, 2nd ed. (Citta del Vatticano: Libreria Editrice Vaticana, 1997), para. 1413.
4. Anthony N. S. Lane, *Justification by Faith in Catholic-Protestant Dialogue: An Evangelical Assessment* (London: T&T Clark, 2002), 223.
5. Ibid.
6. Ibid., 104–105.
7. Ibid., 242.

8. There is also Joseph A. Fitzmyer, for instance, who argues in his exegesis of Romans 3:28 that "in this context Paul means [to teach justification] 'by faith alone.'" Fitzmyer also provides support for *sola fide* from patristic and medieval interpreters. *Romans* (New York: Doubleday, 1993), 360–363. And the Annex (2.C.) to the Joint Declaration on the Doctrine of Justification between the Lutheran World Federation and the Roman Catholic Church states, "Justification takes place 'by grace alone' …, by faith alone; the person is justified 'apart from works'" (Grand Rapids: Eerdmans, 2000), 45.

9. Pope Benedict XVI, *Saint Paul* (San Francisco: Ignatius Press), 82.

10. Ibid., 84.

11. *Catechism of the Catholic Church*, 2nd ed., para. 2017.

12. Peter Kreeft, "Ecumenical Jihad," in *Reclaiming the Great Tradition*, ed. James S. Cutsinger (Downers Grove, Ill.: InterVarsity, 1997), 27.

13. *Catechism of the Catholic Church*, 2nd ed., para. 2041–2043.

14. To be precise, the class was actually at Harvard Divinity School, but the classmates with whom I spent most of my time discussing theology were visiting doctoral students from Boston College.

15. John Owen, *The Doctrine of Justification by Faith*, chapter VII, "Imputation, and the Nature of It." Banner of Truth, *Works*, vol. 5 (Edinburgh: Banner of Truth, 1998), 163–164; quoted in John Piper, *The Future of Justification* (Wheaton, Ill.: Crossway, 2007), 25.

16. Martin Luther, quoted in Gustaf Aulen, *Reformation and Catholicity*, trans. Eric H. Wahlstrom (Edinburgh: Oliver and Boyd, 1962), 76.

17. John Calvin and Jacopo Sadoleto, *A Reformation Debate: Sadoleto's Letter to the Genevans and Calvin's Reply*, ed. John. C. Olin (New York: Harper Torchbooks, 1966), 69.

18. Charles Hodge's Letter to Pope Pius IX. http://banneroftruth.org/us/resources/articles/2010/charles-hodges-letter-to-pope-pius-ix/ (accessed July 24, 2014).

19. J. Gresham Machen, *Christianity and Liberalism* (New York: Macmillan, 1923), 52.

20. John Stott, *Issues Facing Christians Today: A Major Appraisal of Contemporary Social and Moral Questions* (Basingstoke: Marshalls, 1984), 2.

21. Tony Lane, "Relating to the Institution of the Roman Catholic Church: Suggestions for the EEA: A Northern Perspective." Unpublished lecture, delivered June 15, 2007. Used with permission.

SCRIPTURE INDEX

SUBJECT INDEX